The Mazdan Way

The Mazdan Way
Essays on the Good Religion for the West

Stephen E. Flowers

Copyright © 2017
by LODESTAR

All rights reserved. No part of this book, either in part or in whole, may be reproduced, transmitted or utilized in any form or by any means electronic, photographic or mechanical, including photocopying, recording, or by any information storage and retrieval system, without the permission in writing from the Publisher, except for brief quotations embodied in literary articles and reviews.

For permissions, or for the serialization, condensation, or for adaptation write the Publisher at the address below.

Published by
LODESTAR
P.O. Box 16
Bastrop, Texas 78602

www.seekthemystery.com

Abbreviations

Av.	Avestan
BCE	Before the Common Era (= B.C.)
Bund.	*Bundahishn*
CE	Common Era (= A.D.)
Pah.	Pahlavi (Middle Persian)
Pers.	Persian
PGM	*Papyri Graecae Magicae* [= Preisendanz, 1973-74]

Acknowledgments

Gratitude goes to my teachers in the Indo-European and Iranian sphere of mentality: Edgar Polomé and Shapur Shahbazi and to the many thinkers and sages who have gone before. A special note of thanks goes to Daniel Shawn Levie who helped edit the book. All errors of form are entirely the responsibility of the author.

Contents

Introduction		ix
A Historical Prelude: A Brief History of Eranshahr		1
I.	The Mazdan Garden	15
II.	The Good Religion	19
III.	Misconceptions	29
	Dualism	30
	Heresies	33
	Zurvanism	34
	Gnosticism	39
	Manicheanism	42
	Mithraism	45
	Mazdakism	53
	Khorrmanis	57
	Conclusion on Misconceptions	59
IV.	Jesus— the Zoroastrian	61
	Mazdan Reinvention of Judaism	62
	The *Magoi* and the Young Jesus	63
	The Meaning and Mission of Jesus	66
	The Lord's Prayer and the Mazdan Way	69
V.	Angels and Demons	72
VI.	The First True Religion	78
VII.	The Nature and Problem of Evil	86
VIII.	Zarathustra and Islam	91
IX.	The Zarathustrian Nietzsche	97
X.	The Purpose of Humanity	103
XI.	Z-Dog	108
XII.	The Mazdan Way: *Humata-Huxta-Hwaršta*	113
Resources		117
Glossary		119
Bibliography		122

Introduction

This may well be the first book you have ever read or possessed which seeks to discuss topics of Zoroastrianism, the Mazdan Way or even Persian or Iranian culture and religious history. This is not unlikely, but this understandably common lack of knowledge of these topics is not the product of mere benign neglect. Rather it has been the agenda of centuries of Western political, religious and cultural leaders to obfuscate their own indebtedness to *Eranshahr* — the Aryan-Realm — as well as promote their own ragtag version of the eternal myths and spiritual principles taught by the Magians, the priests of the Zoroastrian religion.

Here you will be presented with a series of short pieces written on various topics of special importance or interest in the Mazdan religion and tradition. This is not a book *about* Zoroastrianism, rather it is a book *of* Mazdan ideas and teachings inspired by Zarathustra and conceived of within the guidelines of Mazdan teaching and tradition.

This book is really not necessarily meant to be read from cover to cover. Rather it is a series of independent essays that can be read in any order that strikes the interest of the reader. It is hoped that the reader will read *all* of the essays as they do form a special whole, but not necessarily a linearly developed one.

One of the main purposes of this book is to dispel a certain number of misconceptions that people commonly have about the history and beliefs of ancient Iran. As a minimal foundation we have provided a very short history of *Eranshahr* to act as an orienteering device for the rest of the book and subsequent studies in Iranian thought.

Beyond this historical survey we explore various topics of high interest and spiritual mystery such as the Zoroastrian garden, the role of the dog in Mazdan life, misconceptions surrounding Zoroastrianism such as dualism, gnosticism, Manicheanism and Mithraism. We address the issue of Jesus and his connections to the Mazdan Way. The Iranian origin of the doctrine of angels is laid out along with an explanation of why and how Zoroastrianism was really the world's first authentic religious teaching. Controversial questions surrounding the problem of evil, the purpose of humanity and the relationship of Zoroastrianism to Islam are tackled. In addition there is an exploration of the surprising links between the German philosopher Nietzsche's ideas and those of his alter ego: "Zarathustra." The last essay is a practical introduction to basic methods of engaging in the Mazdan Way.

Many of the essays in this book involve comparative studies or references to things outside the mainstream of Mazdan thought. This approach is often necessary in order that the reader be introduced to central truths by way of more familiar side streets. Our own culture has become lost in a maze of side streets, none seeming to lead back to the central essence of reality. We are encouraged to wander the dark alleyways and avenues, slowly being seduced into the false belief that there is nothing more to discover. Here we shall explore some dark passages, but I hope the central light will always be kept in mind.

For a more general introduction to the religion in question we recommend the book entitled *The Good Religion* (Lodestar, 2014) as a systematic approach to the Mazdan Religion and to the Occidental Temple of the Wise Lord, a Western religious organization dedicated to the practice of religion based on Zarathustran principles for the West.

A Historical Prelude: A Brief History of *Eranshahr*

The Iranian world was many times larger than the modern-day state of Iran. There are many branches to the Iranian family of languages/cultures spreading over a wide geographical space and over a vast expanse of time. At one time (ca. 500 BCE) this realm encompassed lands from eastern Europe to the borders of India.

In this brief history of Eranshahr before 1500 we can only emphasize the basic phases of the history of this enormous culture and highlight several of the major cultural and linguistic groups within this culture. The purpose of this historical prelude is to give a context for the ideas discussed in this book and to provide readers with a sense of orientation within this often bewildering garden of historical delights.

As most readers are probably aware, the Iranians are a subset of the Indo-European cultural and linguistic world. It is known that some six thousand years ago or so there was a group of people who spoke a single language, or a set of dialects so closely related that they were mutually intelligible, and from this prehistoric body of people a whole array of current languages and cultures were derived: the Indic, Iranian, Tocharian, Armenian, Hittite, Slavic, Germanic, Celtic, Hellenic and Italic. So the ancient Greeks, Romans, Gauls, Germans, Slavs, Indians and Persians are all related, all descended, linguistically and culturally from the same root or trunk. This explains their similarities in language, religion, myth and culture and the special relationships (both cooperative and antagonistic) that these cultures have had with each other over the millennia. They all belong to a single ancient family.

The original homeland of the Indo-Europeans was most probably the forests and steppes of what is now the Ukraine, north of the Black Sea and west of the Caspian. They were the first to domesticate the horse and to use the wheel. They were among the first to smelt harder metals, such as copper and bronze. They had a particular social organization led by judge-kings and poet-magicians, populated with warriors and supported by providers and craftsmen. This tripartite social organization was mirrored by the mythic social order of their gods and goddesses.

From early on the Indo-Europeans, or as some called themselves, Aryans, were capable of migrating over vast expanses of space, propelled by their horses and able to move considerable amounts of equipment in wagons over land. They migrated to Asia Minor (present-day Turkey) and Europe to the west and beyond the Caspian Sea to the east. The eastern branch, called Indo-Iranians, first coalesced to the east of the Caspian Sea and from them the Indic branch split off and went further eastward into what is now India. The Proto-Iranians remained in this region around the Caspian and Aral Seas for a time. It was during this period that the Prophet Zarathustra lived. In this homeland there was already friction between pastoralists who herded cattle and rode horses across the steppes and the agriculturally based farmers who lived in the vicinity of urbanized areas. There were early cities in the region of the Oxus River.

Just before approximately 1000 BCE, while some of the Iranian peoples continued a nomadic life and spread out to the north across the steppes, others made their way to the south and west. Those to the north became the North Iranians, the Scythians, Sarmatians and Alans in the northeast and the Kurds and Parthians to the northwest. At the same time some others remained in the region of the original homeland and are the basis of the East Iranians (Sogdians, Sakas), while still others began to migrate to the southwest and onto what is now called the Iranian Plateau of modern-day Iran. These became the South Iranians (Medes, Persians).

In the north there were wide open spaces and few other peoples with whom to compete. Later formidable challenges would come from the Turkic and Mongolian peoples who learned the ways of the horse-culture from the North-Iranian clans. To the south and west, however, the early Iranians immediately confronted the well-established civilizations of the Elamites and Assyrians.

The Achaemenids

The Medes and Persians were closely related groups who settled on the land of what is now Iran. The Medes settled to the west and north, while the Persians lived in the center and south of the land, near the Elamites. A wide ranging kingdom was first established by the Medes stretching from the borders of what is now Turkey to the Indus River in the east. This was unified with the Persian kingdom by Cyrus the Great who formulated the first great Persian Empire named for his house, the Achaemenids. This Achaemenid Empire would last for over three hundred years. At its height this realm encompassed well over twenty different countries and kingdoms which included Egypt, Libya, Babylonia, Assyria, Israel, Thrace, Ionia, Cappadocia, Macedonia, Armenia, Anshan, Parthia, Media, Lydia, Bactria, Sogdia, Gandaria, Saka, Scythia, Ethiopia, India (northwest) and many more. This was the world's first true empire with an emperor, a king of kings (Pers. *shâhânshâh*), governing a far-flung network of quasi-independent kingdoms. Cyrus (Pers. *korush*) would rule from his ceremonial capital in Pasargadae for 31 years, until his death in battle against the northern Iranian Massagetae. Cyrus was so great a leader and visionary that even his enemies, for example the Greeks, deemed him the paragon of leadership— the ideal ruler. It was said that men followed him because they wanted to do so, and nations wanted to be under his rule. He won many battles when the enemy willingly surrendered to him. This is how he conquered Babylon. The Babylonians had heard of Cyrus' kind and generous policies toward those he vanquished, the Babylonians were weary of their oppressive kings and so they willingly opened the gates to the advancing Persian army. When Cyrus addressed the conquered city, the people expected that they might be enslaved, instead Cyrus told them they were free and did not claim victory in the name of his own god, Ahura Mazda, but credited the Babylonian god Marduk with giving him the power to govern Babylon. We know from inscriptions that Cyrus did credit Ahura Mazda with his power to rule, yet his understanding of the one supreme god allowed him to see that other men's gods were but reflections of the one divine glory. At the same time, politically and psychologically, if Cyrus expressed his ideas in terms the conquered people were ready to hear and could understand, he knew he could communicate with the people and make them understand his wishes more clearly. He consciously wanted to establish a new way of governing, based on the concept of wisdom. Cyrus also famously liberated the Jewish people who were held in captivity in Babylon at the time. He allowed them to return to Jerusalem and financed the rebuilding of their temple there. He also used Jewish troops to administer parts of his empire, for example in Elephantine in Egypt. It was a general Persian practice not to send Persians to rule in the conquered nations, but rather to let them rule themselves and forces needed to control any rebellions were usually made up of troops from other nations (foreign legions, if you will) not Persians. This way the Persians could, in general, maintain their prestige as being "above the fray" and not involved in any sort of oppressive activity.

Cyrus' rule was followed by a series of less magnificent, yet usually very capable, emperors. Cambyses II (530-522) took the throne by killing his brother Bardiya. He then defeated the Egyptians at the Battle of Pelusium in 525 and brought Egypt, Libya and Nubia into the Persian Empire. Egypt would be a part of the Persian Empire for long stretches between 525 and 332 BCE and the Persian Emperor would rule as the Pharaoh during the 27th and 31st Dynasties of Egypt. A sorcerer named Gaumata assumed the identity of the dead Bardiya and staged a revolt in Egypt. While this uprising continued, Cambyses died in Syria. Darius I (Daryavaush) [522-486] then came to power and killed Gaumata and at once carried out campaigns in Egypt to expand the empire there and went on to widen Persian territories in the east pushing to the Indus River and beyond the Oxus and Jaxartes in the northeast. Most fatefully he crossed the Bosporus and brought Thrace and Macedonia north of the Greek city states into the empire. A punitive raid against the Greek states was thwarted at Marathon (490) by the Athenians. Darius died as he prepared to campaign further against the Greeks.

Darius I was also given the moniker "the Great." It was he who really designed the Persian Empire as a work of state craft based on the foundations of Cyrus and fueled by the philosophy of Zarathustrianism. He finished the ceremonial and political center known as Persepolis, "City of the Persians." Works of civil engineering, such as a system of subterranean aqueducts were completed. These brought a steady supply of water to the desert plains. Roads were developed throughout the empire. A currier system was used which kept the emperor in close contact with all areas of his far-flung realm. Herodotus wrote of this "pony-express" system:

> It is said that as many days as there are in the whole journey, so many are the men and horses that stand along the road each horse and man at the interval of a day's journey, and these are stayed neither by snow nor rain nor heat nor darkness from the accomplishing their appointed course with all speed.
>
> *Histories* 8.98

Darius was succeeded by his son Xerxes (Khashayarsha) I 486-465 who continued the conflict with Greece. The Achaemenid Empire included many Greek-speaking areas in what is now Turkey and the Balkan Peninsula. It was in defense of these areas against disruptive Greek city-states, e.g. Athens and Sparta, that the Persians first started to come into conflict with Greece proper. Thus began the fateful Greco-Persian Wars (500-479 BCE). This conflict featured two major campaigns of the Persians invading the heart of the Greek homeland. The first ended at the Battle of Marathon (490 BCE) when the Athenians defeated a Persian army, which returned to the Persian Empire over the Aegean Sea. In the second campaign a Persian army of 100,000 men, led by the emperor Xerxes himself, crossed the Bosporus into Greece. They were famously delayed in September of 490 by a relatively small contingent of 300 Spartans along with 5,600 other troops, at Thermopylae. The Persians conquered Athens, sacked the city and occupied the Greek heartland for ten years. Then the Greeks won the naval battle at Salamis (480 BCE) and eventually the Persians retreated back to Asia Minor. In the end the Greek city-states of Athens and Sparta won the struggle to free themselves of Persian influence and proceeded to tear each other apart.

Culturally and historically we usually only hear the Greek side of this history. It is couched in terms of West *versus* East, freedom and virtue *versus* tyranny and decadence. This model of propagandistic understanding reverberates to this day because it worked so well. In point of fact the Persian Empire allowed its constituent kingdoms great freedom and provided for their peaceful existences and interactions. Several Greek city-states had willingly joined the Persian Empire. On the other hand most of the other Greek city-states were constantly at war with each other and falling into tyranny both from within and without in a chaotic historical melodrama.

One of the great myths of history, and one we see played out in historical as well as other media accounts of these times, is that the confrontation between Greece and Iran was one between freedom and tyranny. Nothing could be further from the truth. One need only look as far as this astonishing cultural fact: Greece was dependent on slavery (half of the people in any Greek city state were slaves) yet slavery was banned in the Persian Empire. Cyrus and other emperors paid their workers and only sold prisoners of war to other slave-holding nations. This aversion to the practice of slavery stems directly from the practice of Zarathustran ethics. There was little that was admirable about Greek democracy: Socrates was "democratically" put to death. Remember that democracy is only two wolves and a sheep voting on what's for dinner.

The Achaemenid Empire was the first true empire in world history and it and its eventual successor Sasanian Empire were the only ones that ever really worked as it was supposed to work. The empires of Alexander and Rome were but pale and dysfunctional shadows of their Persian models and natural rivals. The great German philosopher Hegel once wrote:

> In Persia first arises that light which shines itself and illuminates what is around. For Zoroaster's "Light" belongs to the World of Consciousness— the Spirit as a relation to something distinct from itself. We see in the Persian World a pure exalted Unity, as the essence which leaves the special existences that inhere in it free;— as the Light, which only manifests what bodies are in themselves;— a Unity which governs individuals only to excite them to become more powerful for themselves — to develop and assert their individuality. ... The principle of development begins with the history of Persia; this constitutes therefore the beginning of history.
>
> *The Philosophy of History*, pp. 173-174

An educational system existed which taught boys from the time they were five to twenty. Herodotus famously says that they learned three things: to ride a horse, to draw a bow and the speak the Truth. The worst thing was to tell a lie, the next worst was to owe a debt (because, it is said, that it leads the debtor to have to lie).

With the wars with the Greeks behind them, the reign of Artaxerxes I (465-424) was marked by relative peace and prosperity. At this time Zoroastrianism becomes the *de facto* religion of state. After the brief reigns of Xerxes II and Sogdianus the emperor Darius II (423-405) came to the throne and prepared the way for Artaxerxes II. The reign of Artaxerxes II (404-358) ushered in forty-five years of peace and prosperity and under this new emperor Zoroastrianism was spread into Asia Minor, Armenia and the Levant as temples are built throughout the empire. These temples never contained any images of the gods and goddesses, so Herodotus tells us, which is confirmed by archeology. His reign was followed by those of Artaxerxes III (358-338) and Artaxerxes IV (338-336) during which time the Persian religion firmly reincorporated many of the old gods and goddesses of the Iranian pantheon such as Mithra and Anahita within a Zarathustran understanding. Greek aesthetic influence and cultural cross-fertilization led to the creation of images for the gods and goddesses at that time.

The Macedonian Conquest

In the kingdom of Macedonia, which had been part of the Persian Empire at one time, a young king ascended to their throne in 336: Alexander. He had been tutored by a fellow Macedonian in his youth: Aristotle. The Macedonians were a Hellenized people, that is they spoke Greek and worshipped the Greek gods, but had their own gods as well which corresponded to the Greek divinities. For the Macedonians were not originally Greeks at all, but from another Indo-European stock, most likely related to the Thracians or Iryllians. Alexander was of two minds about the Persians, on the one hand he wanted to avenge Macedon and Greece on them and defeat them as the main cultural rivals of the Hellenic world, yet on the other hand he admired the Persians as did many thinking Greeks both for their philosophy and their proven ability to rule a vast empire. Alexander in fact consciously modeled himself and his ambitions on the accomplishments of Cyrus the Great. He learned of these things from Xenophon's book about Cyrus entitled the *Cyropedia* (written about 370 BCE).

First Alexander subdued all the Greek city-states, then marched into the Persian Empire and defeated the Persian army under Darius III at Issus and then moved on to conquer Egypt, removing it and its resources from the Persian Empire. Then he moved further east into the empire defeating the Persians in the battle of Gaugamela in 331. Darius fled to the eastern part of the empire and was later assassinated by the head of his personal guard, Bessus. Alexander occupied Persepolis and was crowned Persian emperor. Persepolis was destroyed to avenge the sacking of Athens. The Macedonian leader then visited the tomb of his hero, Cyrus, at Pasagardae. He found it had been looted of its riches by the Greeks! Alexander's megalomaniacal plan was to unify the Greek and Persian aristocracies and to form a ruling race of men. He arranged marriages for his men to Persian women and he himself took at least two Persian brides. In general Persian court ritual was adopted by the

Macedonians and the process of Persianization had begun. Alexander unexpectedly died at the age of thirty-three after a bout of heavy drinking. The empire of the Persians had been effectively conquered by this Macedonian king due to a combination of inner turmoil in Persia coupled with the military and visionary genius of Alexander. History calls him "great," but he was not great in the same way as Cyrus. Alexander's was a soul of violence and excess which often clouded his judgment. Upon his death the empire, now called the Seleucid Empire, was divided into satrapies generally at first ruled by Macedonian generals. Greek replaced Aramaic as the language of commerce and government. In the cities and along trade routes Greek and Persian ideas mingled, yet in the countryside and especially in the mountains the Zoroastrian faith continued uninterrupted.

A word should be said about language in the Persian Empire. There was in Iran, as in other Indo-European cultures, a general traditional disdain for the written word. Real knowledge was something that was learned orally from master to pupil and memorized. This was true from India to Ireland, and it was at first no less true in Iran. The ancient Zoroastrian texts were not written at first, but memorized. Writing was used for various purposes, e.g. records, governmental policies, laws, and decrees. A modified form of cuneiform writing was used for short inscriptions in Old Persian, for example. However, in general other languages were used for writing, especially Elamite and Aramaic. After Alexander Greek was used for a few centuries, but the oral tradition continued unaltered through these centuries. Later, in the time of the Sasanian Empire (224-651 CE) new alphabets were developed to commit both the Avestan sacred hymns and their translations and commentaries along with other sacred works in the contemporary language of Pahlavi. This commitment to writing had some of the negative effects that the wise ancients had predicted: the people became increasingly dependent on the written word and when the books were later partially destroyed and lost, so too was the knowledge lost and fragmented. However, without this written record, all would have eventually been lost to us.

The Macedonians ruled in Persia for about a century, but their court was largely Persianized fairly quickly. As a result Persian ideas penetrated into the West through Greece far more than western ideas did so in Iran. The "imperial idea" spread to Greece and then to Rome. Most historical accounts we have of Alexander were written by Greeks and later Romans who idealized him. The Persians generally had a more negative and realistic view of him as a brute, tyrant and practitioner of every excess, later Persian texts would call him *guzastag*— "the accursed."

The Seleucids and Parthians

The first satrap of the post-Alexander regime was Seleucus Nictor, who ruled mainly from the western part of the satrapy in Babylon. His name gave an identity to the Seleucid Empire, which at first encompassed most of the old Persian Empire. The stronghold of the Seleucids was in the far western part of the empire in what is now Syria and Iraq. However, to the east in what is now Afghanistan and as early as about 248 BC, the Arsacid Dynasty arose from among northeastern Iranian horsemen. This was led by Arshak (Arsaces) who consolidated power among the Parthians. Although the Arsacids were descended from nomads, but they increasingly adopted the trappings of Persian culture. From this incursion there developed a Parthian Empire which over the span of two centuries was able to overcome the Seleucids in the west and take over most of the old Persian territories including Mesopotamia. Mithradates I declared himself *Shâhânshâh* in 123 BCE, and so the idea and reality of a Persian Empire was renewed. These Parthians became the chief rivals of the Romans in their efforts to expand their own influence eastward. Mainly they fought over Armenia, Syria and Mesopotamia. For the most part these wars were stalemates, with the Iranians usually retaining at least nominal control over these regions. This Roman/Persian conflict would extend well into the time of the Sasanians with similar results. The Parthians ruled with a light hand on their peoples, allowing the different areas to govern themselves for the most part. Their empire would last almost five hundred years.

The pattern was established by which Persia would be conquered by foreign invaders and then after a more or less short period of time the Persian culture — political, philosophical, economic, spiritual — would reassert itself from within. This was mainly because the Persian idea of organization was superior to that of all conquerers. Therefore in order to be able to govern the land they had conquered the invaders had to adapt themselves to the Persian way. This pattern would be repeated after the Arab / Muslim invasion as well as those of the Turks and various Mongol incursions.

The Sasanian Empire

The Empire of the Parthians was a fairly decentralized government. It lacked many of the organizational principles which had characterized the Achaemenid Empire. Out of the old Persian heartland of Pars there arose a new ruling house: the Sasanians. After a local ruler named Papak started the process around 205, Ardashir, the first Sasanian ruler consolidated power and was eventually crowned the new Persian King of Kings in 224 as Ardashir I (224-242) after defeating the Parthians at the Battle of Hormozgan. By the time of his death he was able to recover much of what had been lost in the time of the Parthians. The Sasanian Empire would last some four hundred and twenty-seven years from 224 to 651 CE.

The history of the Sasanian Empire is divided into five eras: the early, the first golden era, an intermediate era, a second golden era, and finally the era of the decline and fall of the empire.

The son of Ardashir, Shahpur I (240-270) became the first great emperor of this new state. He expanded and consolidated the territories of the empire and successfully combated the Romans in the west. Most notably he defeated the Romans at the Battle of Edessa capturing the Roman Emperor Valerian along with thousands of Romans and their auxiliaries from various European tribes, including many Germans, and resettled them in the cities of Gandishapur and Bishapur where they lived in peace as "guests" of the Persian emperor sharing their knowledge and building many civil engineering projects, some of which still stand today.

The reign of Shapur I was characterized by religious tolerance as well as a renewal and expansion of the Good Religion. The most notable example of his religious tolerance is the fact that he allowed the religious artist and innovator, Mani, to preach his heretical faith at court and throughout the empire. The ideas of Mani are discussed in some detail in essay III in this book. In general Shapur was followed by a series of less able and less tolerant emperors.

Zoroastrianism underwent significant reforms during Sasanian times. The use of writing was enthusiastically embraced, whereas it had been suspect as a daevic influence before. The religious works were committed to writing in a special alphabet called the *Dîn Daberah*, "Alphabet for Religion." It was a perfectly phonetic script containing over fifty characters in which any dialect could be written. Works of religion were recorded and codified. (Some of this material has been lost due to disruptions caused by the Muslim invasion and its aftermath.) Rituals were elaborated and expanded under the influence of a well-established, professional priesthood. Shorter rituals were combined to create longer and more complex ones. The priesthood itself gained in power and authority as the Good Religion was for the first time established as the official religion of state.

The Sasanian Empire remained religiously very diverse with Zoroastrianism as the dominant faith, yet with sizable minorities of Christians (Babylonian or Nestorian), Jews, Manicheans, Mandaens, Mithrists, traditional Iranian pagans, as well as Hindus and Buddhists in the eastern part of the empire. Occasionally some of these other faiths would come under scrutiny and suspicion, as they were seen to be connected to external, hostile states, especially Rome.

Shapur II (309-379) defined the first golden era of Sasanian history. He was a capable military leader and a brilliant organizer and designer of social policies. His reign was followed by what is called the intermediate period which is characterized by relative peace and prosperity largely engendered by the continuation of policies established by Shapur II.

During this time the capital of Rome was moved to Byzantium, later renamed Constantinople (now Istanbul). Rome itself was falling into decay and would soon be overtaken by the Germanic tribes.

After this high point in the history of the empire under Shapur II there followed a period of weak rulers which began the intermediate era between the two golden ages. The first ruler of note during this time was Yazdegerd I (399-421). He was a tolerant protector of minorities who made peace with the Romans and married a Jewish princess. Their son, Bahram V (421-438) was a brilliant emperor whose reign was the high point of the intermediate period. He sponsored the arts and literature and introduced the formal sport of polo, which spread beyond the frontiers of the empire. After a span of weak rulers, Kavadh I came to power in 488.

At first Kavadh I gave support to the radical reformer Mazdak. Among these reforms were the sharing of land and women by the hereditary aristocracy. Because of the sizable harems of the leading aristocrats, there were not enough women to go around. Also there was the peculiar practice of next-of-kin marriage designed to keep property tightly controlled by families. Other beliefs and practices of the proto-socialist Mazdakites were free love, hedonism, vegetarianism, a rule of no-killing, and very liberal customs of hospitality. For his support of Mazdak Kavadh was ousted and replaced by the benevolent Djamasp (496-498). In 498 Kavadh returned to reclaim his throne, which Djamasp peacefully ceded. During the second reign of Kavadh I military action was taken against the Mazdakites and the reformer and many of his supporters were killed.

Although the Mazdakite movement was suppressed the ideas and secret networks of adherents to these ideas would persist in secret for centuries to come. The quasi-Islamic sect of the Khorramis is based on Mazdakite doctrines. The radical reforms proposed by the Mazdakite movement had their effects on orthodox Zoroastrianism and the Persian establishment. As a system of *creative evolution* Zoroastrianism is open to change and improvement without compromising its basic and eternal principles.

As regards foreign policy, the Sasanian Empire carried on good and productive relations with both China and India throughout its history. The peaceful coexistence with the empires of the far east tends to demonstrate that it was the bellicose nature of the Romans which was at the root of the centuries of war between the West and East.

The second golden era was in full swing by the reign of Khorasaw I (531-579), who was a great reformer of governmental institutions, bringing greater revenues and centralizing the government and military command. He also affirmed Zoroastrianism as the state religion. After a setback during the time of Hormizd IV, the emperor Khosrow II (590-628) would be the last truly great emperor of the Sasanian Empire. At one point he was forced to flee the country and made an alliance with the Byzantine emperor, Maurice, and regained the throne. In 602 Maurice was murdered, throwing the Byzantine Empire into chaos. Khosrow takes advantage of this and invades the West and retakes vast territories, including Egypt. The war with Byzantium would last until 628.

Arabic Conquest and Islam

The Sasanian Empire was being economically and militarily exhausted in the beginning of the seventh century. There were internal rivalries and administration was becoming weak, as was military organization. The protracted war with the Byzantines was draining resources, a plague killed half of the population of western Iran in 628, after which a civil war broke out. In 632 Yazdegerd III became emperor. Normally this would have been part of a cyclical phase until a new and vital leader would revive the traditions of wealth production, military might and wise administration. However, into this point of weakness there was a new a storm brewing in the west: an Arabian prophet of a new religion (Islam) named Mohammed had formed a fighting force that conquered the lands to the west and south of Iran. After the death this leader and in the same year Yazdegerd III had been crowned Mohammed's successors, along with some Iranian allies, invaded the Sasanian Empire. Yazdegerd fled to the east together with the whole Sasanian court and a core of warriors. The emperor was murdered in Merv, and his son, along with the court went into exile in Teng China where they served the Chinese emperor and became part of the Chinese military establishment.

After a struggle of some fifteen years the Arabs fully overcame the empire and established the Umayyad Caliphate (651-750). During this time it is estimated that only about ten percent of Iranians converted to Islam. At first Islam was tantamount to "the Arab religion." In fact, conversion was not made easy by the Arabs because non-Muslims were taxed at a higher rate and so having many non-Muslims in the caliphate was a significant source of revenue. By the end of this period the Persians began to transform Islam from within by imbuing it with increasing Iranian features and ideas. It is under Persian influence that Islam is mutated from the Arabic code into an international and universal religion. In 750 the Umayyads were overthrown and the Abbasid Caliphate was established. This caliphate would last three centuries until the middle of the eleventh century. It was during this time that Persian ideology was well-established in the Islamic world. At this time Sasanian culture made an enormous impact on Islamic ideas, customs and practices. It can be said that almost every aspect of what we now think of as "Islamic" culture— especially music, art, architecture, mathematics, philosophy, etc., was either directly borrowed from, or heavily influenced by, Sasanian culture. By the end of this period the Persian language even began being used as a philosophical language.

The indigenous Iranian culture continued to be a matrix for the fomentation of revolt and rebellion against the Abbisids for another century. In the 750s a coalition of Zoroastrians, Khorramites and Shi'ites known as the *Surkh-jâmagân*, "red-clad ones," rebelled against the Abbisids under Abu Muslim, and then in the early 800s Bâbak Khorramdîn (795-838) fought the caliphate for twenty years before he was betrayed and executed.

At the beginning of the Abbasid caliphate about forty percent of Persians were Muslims, by the end of this time that number had risen to about ninety-eight percent. The success of Islam was keyed to its increasingly Iranianized nature. Zoroastrianism remained a minority religion, as it does today.

After the age of revolts the old religion of Zoroastrianism survived more quietly in the countryside and in the mountains, especially around Yazd. But the key to survival was becoming unobtrusive and almost invisible.

Sometime during the middle of the tenth century a group of Zoroastrians left Iran and migrated to the coast of India, in the vicinity of modern-day Mombai. There they set up a new community and maintained occasional linkages with their co-religionists in Iran over the centuries. These Zoroastrians in India are known as Parsis and it is among them that the religion continued to thrive most vigorously, free from persecution.

Persian culture was extended further into Central Asia among the Turkic peoples and further eastward into the Indian Subcontinent at this time. It was through the agency of the Persians that various Turkic peoples were Islamicized. Iran absorbed, and as a matter of course "Persianized," many often brutal invasions by the Turkic tribes and Mongols in the subsequent centuries. At the dawn of the modern age, in 1502, Ismail I was crowned the first Shah of the Shi'ite New Persian Empire, known as the Safavid Empire, which would last until 1722.

A Postscript on Modern History

As bad as the invasions of Turks and Mongols had been, the culture had continued to thrive even in these times of upheaval. But the Safavids, who established Shi'ism as the official state form of religion and who were themselves of Turkic background, speaking a Turkic language at court, ushered in the worst of times in Iranian history. Damage done to the culture during these times of despotism and intolerance are still strongly felt today.

It is a general misconception that Shi'ism is a peculiarly Iranian form of Islam and that it is somehow represents a special survival of Iranian ideas within Islam. This is basically not true. In fact Sunni Islam itself was heavily influenced by Iranian ideas and practices from an early date, and after the ninth century Iranian ideas flooded into the Islamic world through the Sufi schools, philosophers and poets of Iran. The establishment of Shi'a Islam in Iran as a factor which separates the Iranian region from other Islamic areas is a fairly modern feature dating from this time of the Safavids (1502-1722). The original stronghold of Shi'ism is not in Iran, but in southern Mesopotamia (Iraq), which was often part of Iranian territory politically.

This is no place to discuss the distinctions between Sunni and Shi'ite versions of Islam in any detail, as it is not important to our major interest. The fall of the Safavid state in 1722 ushered in an even more despotic, cruel and violent chapter of history greatly at odds with the Persian spirit of tolerance and enlightenment. Iran progressively came under the influence of foreign states, especially Britain and Russia who played what came to be called "The Great Game" in the region. As the Persian state became weaker, the power of the Shi'ite clerics grew.

Although there were many cultural accomplishments by Persian men of letters and philosophers, and the Persianized form of Islam known as Sufism was developed, the Iranians would never again rise to the level of cultural influence and power they had had in the Zoroastrian Ages of the Achaemenid, Parthian and Sasanian Empires. Islam brought corrupt, cruel and decadent leadership to the land and increasingly, instead of being an exporter of cultural and ideological material, the land came under foreign influence and domination. The grip of Islam and the Shi'ite mullahs tightened and the past glories of Zoroastrian Iran faded from the memories of the masses.

The twentieth century saw a new player enter the Great Game, the United States. These foreign players set up a new ruling family in Iran, which came to be called the Pahlavi dynasty. The major draw for these players were the oil reserves to be found in Iran. The Soviet Revolution in Russia began to spill out into Persia. To counter this the British overthrew the Qajar dynasty and installed an obscure commander of a Cossack brigade as shah: Reza Khan Pahlavi (1926-1941). He embarked on a modernization campaign and ruled until he became too friendly with the National Socialists in Germany. Forced to abdicate, his son became shah.

The reign of Mohammed Reza Pahlavi (1941-1979) was marked by accelerated modernization programs, a fascination with the glories of the Iranian imperial past, a generally friendly attitude toward the state of Israel, and a dedication to containing the power of the ultra-conservative Islamic clerics, or mullahs, in Iran. The shah was hated by both the far left Communists in his country, as well as the Shi'ite imams. These leftists and religious zealots were in agreement about only one thing: the shah and the culture he was attempting to (re)establish had to go.

It was estimated that the shah had as many as five thousand political prisoners in his jails and his attempts to suppress these dissident forces were considered harsh by Western standards. He would quietly insist that his critics simply "did not understand" the *nature* of his opposition. In 1979 American politicians, led by a marginally qualified peanut farmer and part-time Baptist preacher, withdrew support for the Shah of Iran who was forced to flee the country as the chief Islamic cleric, the Ayatollah Khomenei, arrived to take control of the land. Soon, and ever since thereafter, the entire world would feel the effects of the forces the embattled shah had attempted to keep at bay. Many of the best elements of Iranian society emigrated to Western lands, but many good people remained as well. Despite the so-called Islamic Revolution it is reported that today less than two percent of Iranians attend Friday prayers.

I. The Mazdan Garden

One of the most conspicuous aspects of Persian culture is the importance of gardens. Formal, symbolic and practical gardens were essential to Iranian culture from the time when the originally nomadic Iranian tribes began to enter the semiarid region to the south and west of their original homeland to the north and east. The whole of the Iranian Plateau slopes from the mountains in the north to the sea in the south. This allowed them to develop an elaborate system of subterranean irrigation tunnels to feed water throughout the land by means of the naturally available power of gravity.

Early kings developed palace complexes which included formal gardens fed by water from tanks high up in the neighboring hills and mountains. This created artificial oases in the arid and desolate countryside— an astounding and seemingly miraculous symbol of kingly wisdom and power. Most importantly, however, it is a sign of the coming transformation of the world from a desolate condition into a happy and verdant one. It is a prefiguration of the Paradise to come.

The word "paradise" comes from Old Persian *paridaiza*, by way of the Greek πααδεισος. It originally referred to a walled or enclosed garden space. The ultimate Paradise unfolds in the world when the final victory of good over evil occurs. This can only happen when Man works together with the Wise Lord to make it so.

As we will see in a later article, the Mazdan Way has nothing to do with the dualism between matter and spirit. According to Mazdan theory matter and spirit, or material manifestation and spiritual archetypes or prototypes are equally good. Both are included in the good and one is not inherently superior to the other. This philosophical principle presses the Mazdan to turn thought into action, good spiritual prototypes into material objects and experiences based on these prototypes endowed with the good. The construction and experience of a Persian Garden is an exercise in this philosophy. It is an idea made manifest, and one that can be directly experienced physically and spiritually at the same time. In this it is the absolute foretaste of Paradise.

The "Garden of Eden"

It is widely acknowledged by religious historians that the so-called Garden of Eden depicted in the Book of Genesis in the Old Testament was based on an Iranian model. The figures appearing in the story: Man, Woman, Serpent, God, and the idea of a garden as the idealized map of the earth are all of Iranian origin. The Jews became familiar with these images during the Babylonian Captivity, from which they were liberated by the Persian Emperor, Cyrus (Koresh) the Great in 539 BCE.

How is the Garden of Eden described in the Book of Genesis? We find it in Chapter 2 of that book where we read:

> 8. And the LORD GOD planted a garden eastward, in Eden; and there He put the man whom He had formed. 9. And out of the ground made the LORD GOD to grow every tree that is pleasant to the sight, and good for food; the tree of life also in the midst of the garden, and the tree of the knowledge of good and evil. 10. And a river went out of Eden to water the garden; and from thence it was parted and became four heads.

The division of a garden into four parts divided by four irrigation channels is the most basic design for a Persian garden, technically referred to as a *chehâr-bagh*, or four-part garden. In the Septuagint, or the Greek version of the Old Testament, the garden is called πααδεισος, that is "paradise." This is a word first used in Greek by Xenophon who wrote a study of Cyrus the Great (*The Cyropedia*). The Persian garden is not only a mirror of a heavenly realm, it is also a ritual gateway between this world and the world of heaven.

In the ruins of many of the ancient cities and/or royal ceremonial centers we find the remains of many of the most ancient gardens in the Iranian world. Ancient cities such as Persepolis, Pasargadae, Ectabana, Darabgerd, and many many other ancient Iranian cities which can be researched. Many were well-planned and laid out, sometimes they were even circular in design. The gardens offered the same thing as our parks and green belts do today.

Elaborate design in the service of urban living and ceremonial spaces was a passion of the ancient Iranians. One of the Seven Wonders of the World was the "Hanging Gardens of Babylon." This complex was built by the Babylonian king Nebuakanezzar II to please his Median wife, Amytis, who was longing for the atmospheres of her homeland. In order that she not become too homesick, the garden complex was designed and built. (Archeological evidence seems to suggest that these gardens were actually in Niniveh.) But it would seem that the practice of elaborate gardens was imported to Mesopotamia from the Iranian world.

The basic Persian garden design went on to find a home in later Islamic culture, though which it spread from India to Spain.

The Basic Design of a Persian Garden

A Mazdan garden can be as simple or as elaborate as resources and interest allow. The main structural characteristics are that it is usually divided into four parts, into four quadrants, divided and watered by a running water course and, if possible a fountain in the center. It should be walled on all sides.

A typical plan would look like:

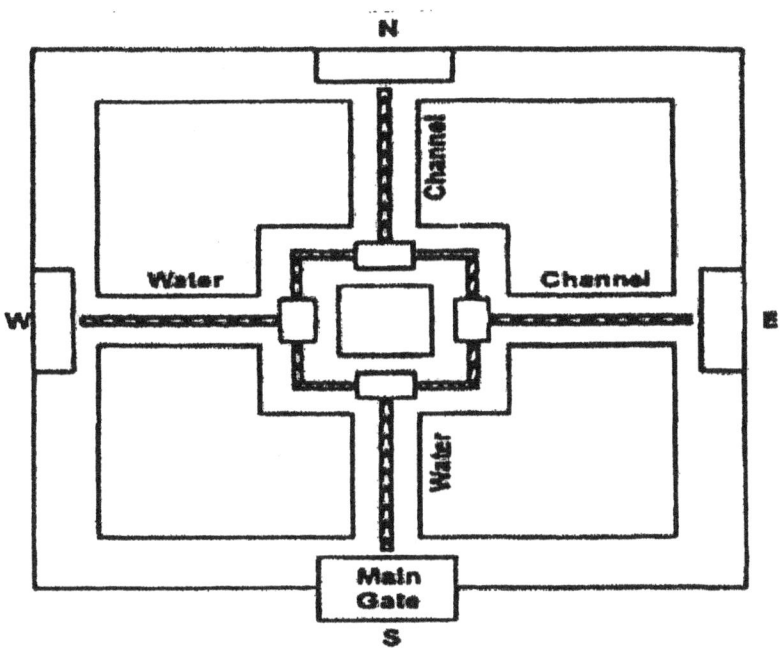

For purposes of practicing the Mazdan Way space should be provided for an altar with provisions for a fire (*afrinigan*) or even a so-called fire element which could provide an eternal flame for the environment.

In general the design is made so that it will provide a cool environment in the heat of the year. The water and plants combine to cool the air and the walls hold this air in and insulate the space from the harsh outside conditions.

It could actually be the calling of a Mazdan person to devote him or herself to the design and construction of Mazdan gardens of all types and sizes as a noble profession. These gardens would be both beautiful places of recreation and spiritual retreats and venues for the performance of holy rites. Research on the Internet about Persian gardens yields copious results.

Spiritual Importance of the Garden

The final earthy paradise which will be established by Ahura Mazda in partnership with Man, the chief terrestrial coworker (*hamkār*) of God, will not be a colorless obliteration of all differences but a Paradisiacal garden of all the species of Creation, including all the magnificent and unique cultural manifestations of mankind's past. The Garden is a symbol of this, and much else besides. Within it all things existed, and will exist in balance and in full bloom of variety.

The building and tending such a garden is an act of magic. By means of the establishment of such a garden the substance of the terrestrial realm is symbolically altered, as well as being materially developed. The quality and symbolism used in the construction and the effort spent in tending the garden have a magical (transformative) effect on the world around the garden and the gardener. Each garden becomes a transmission station for the radiant power of Ahura Mazda in the world.

A Mazdan garden works subtly on the world around it, but also in a more direct way it works on the minds of the people who tend it, meditate, contemplate and worship within its environs. It also works on the minds of those who might step into its space and experience it directly. It is an instrument of objective change and a tool for subjective, or inner, development.

II. The Good Religion

Introducing the Mazdan Way

The Good Religion is dawning once more in a world in need. You can experience a new day in the spirit with the realization of wisdom in your life and remembering who you really are. The Good Religion stems from an ancient source, a source which fed all of the so-called great religions of history. This source has been hidden from most, yet has lived in the open, unseen. Now is the time to open our eyes and receive the light of the world. Its beliefs may seem familiar, but its story is mysterious. This is because a return to the hidden source of anything will always give that feeling which welds together surprising insight and familiar comfort.

The Good Religion teaches that there is only one God, called by the name Wise Lord— who is pure focused consciousness. This is the true God, beyond all characteristics of anger, fear, or jealousy. Whom we do not fear, and who is a friend and comrade of all humanity. Who wants you to be happy, strong and wise; prosperous, secure and intelligent. Beyond this the Wise Lord loves and respects humanity so much that mankind is taken into the Lord's confidence and made a coworker and comrade in the great and divine project: the perfection of the world.

At the time of the origin of the universe, dark shadows appeared— filled with lack, weakness and ignorance. Within these crevices were bred entities which rose to challenge the divine order. The Wise Lord, all-seeing in wisdom, knew of this and created Seven Creations: Sky, Water, Earth, Plants, Cattle, Man and Fire to oppose the forces and patterns of evil. Evil is characterized by deficiency and excess, in a word *imbalance*. This force infected all of the Creations and introduced the Lie. Examples of the Lie are that the spirit is mortal, that humans were created by a violent and vengeful god, and that wisdom and knowledge should be shunned in favor of blind obedience.

Of the Seven Creations the most important is Man. Only Man living in the midst of the world can act as a creative partner with God. Man is charged with the task of helping to guard and develop the other six Creations— as well as himself.

Humanity was created when God called for volunteers from among the spiritual beings (*fravashis*) in heaven to become materialized on Earth in order to assist God in the forthcoming battle against the Lie. The angelic beings all volunteered to become men and women. Therefore all men and women living in the world today are here through an original choice for the Good, although through infection by the Lie they have largely forgotten their true heritage. Remembrance of the Truth is one of our greatest needs.

The individual human being engages in the war on evil by practicing a three-fold path of *humata-hukhta-hwarshta*: Good Thoughts, Good Words and Good Actions.

All humans are naturally born as Mazdans. People do not "convert" to the Good Religion so much as they Remember their spiritual identities and revert back to the Mazdan Way.

Traditional Religion Perfected

For decades groups have been attempting to revive or reawaken religions based on ancient organic values— the Celtic, Norse, Germanic, Roman, Greek or Slavic. All of these folk-groups stem from a single trunk— that of the Indo-Europeans. A visionary few longed for a revival of a Pan-Indo-European religion. The astounding fact is that such a system already exists. More amazing still, it has existed for almost four thousand years. This is the religious philosophy and theology of the founder of the world's first universal, trans-tribal, or international, religion: the first and only necessary Prophet, Zarathustra. Zarathustra, or Zoroaster as the Greeks called him, was a pagan priest of the Indo-European religion as practiced in the first half of the second millennium BCE— nearly 4,000 years ago. He was specifically a *zaotar*-type priest. It is said that when he was born, instead of crying, as most babies do, he laughed out loud because he was filled with the glory that was to come. As an adult he was the first to envision One God — the God of Consciousness — as being the first god-form from which all other divine principles, or gods, are derived. This god he called Lord Wisdom (Ahura Mazda). More specifically this is the god of pure focused consciousness. The designation of "Ahura Mazda" was a singular and new formula which reflected the unique and original insight of the Prophet. Zarathustra was then the first to see the traditional gods and goddesses as *abstract principles*. Mithra was not merely the god of contracts, he is the *principle* of the contract itself. As such he became the world's first true philosopher, as well as its first theologian and true prophet. Whenever clever men of antiquity first heard the message of Zarathustra they were immediately struck by the profound insight it provided, and they were forever transformed. It is important to remember that his original vision is really a refinement of the pagan Indo-European ideology, not a rejection of it. Parts of his vision eventually would become models for most of the world's so-called great religions— Judaism, Buddhism, Christianity and Islam. Zoroastrianism can be said to be a philosophized and universalized version of pagan Indo-European thought. It is sophisticated, abstract thought based on Indo-European ideas and made to be a system to which any and all persons or nations in the world could belong as a matter of free individual *choice.* The age and level of Zarathustra's system also makes it a Pan-Indo-European one, one which existed at a time before the divisions into Germans, Celts, Greeks, Romans, Iranians and Indians were very great at all.

By utilizing Zarathustra's methods as a guide we can easily and logically manifest a system for the universal renewal of an Indo-European religion of universal application. This is called the Occidental Temple of the Wise Lord.

Ahura Mazda is not just the god of Zarathustra's people, but of all peoples of the world. Many other subsequent religions would be influenced by his insights and those of later Zoroastrian sages, either directly or indirectly. After his flash of insight this first prophet of a true religion began to compose a series of short texts called the Gathas, many of which survive to us today as the bedrock of the religion of Zoroastrianism. These texts and others composed in the ancient language known as Avestan, can have a transformative effect on human consciousness through a combination of their sound and meaning. They are called *manthras.*

Dawning of a New Age

The world exists in a perpetual state of anticipation of the coming of something new. Unexpectedly the newest way is coming from roots of the oldest religious tradition in the world— Zoroastrianism. A prophecy says that their will be a flash of light coming from the east to the west. This will have its inception sometime around 2012-2014, It is in this timeframe that the Occidental Temple of the Wise Lord— or the Mazdan Faith for the West was founded. This spiritual path is the oldest known religion— that is, a universal set of beliefs and values available to all human kind not restricted in its validity to a certain tribe or nation, which you have to choose free of all threats of violence or coercion. The emerging western Mazdan tradition offers a full range of religious and esoteric practices and methods. Most of these have been cultivated in the East for millennia, but have only made their ways to the West in garbled and ignorant forms. After all, the very word "Magic(k)" is derived from the title of one grade of Zoroastrian priests, the *magûs.* We now have the opportunity to be cultivators of these newest and oldest forms of practice in meditation, personal ritual, esoteric prayer, spiritual development— as well as positive social action in the physical and cultural environment.

Much is made of "magic." Most do not know that the word comes from the Persian *magû,* or *magavan,* a class of priests among them. They practiced the truest form of magic— and rejected all sorcery as unnecessary. Their original form of pure magic elevates the being of the practitioner through a system of ritualized, symbolic, intellectual and ethical thoughts, words and deeds. At the end of the journey all is provided for and happiness is gained.

The Mazdan Jesus

Everyone is familiar with the Christian Nativity scene, a favorite Christmas tradition, the crèche display. Always essential to the scene is the appearance of the three "wise men," identified as *magoi* or *magi* in the Greek and Latin Gospels. These *magi* were, of course, Zoroastrian priests who had "followed a star" from their home in the Parthian Empire to recognize Jesus as a newborn Savior. In their tradition a series of Saviors, or Saoshyants, would be born at various points in history to bring the message of the Good Religion of universal salvation. The presence of the *magi* in the Gospel of Matthew both indicates the place of Jesus in their tradition as well as declares their approval of Jesus as a Savior. This point was important to many Jews in the time of Jesus, as the Persians were seen as the leading light of religious thought. The Pharisees were originally the "Persian faction" of Judaism of that age. Judaism had been greatly reformed under Persian influence at the time that Cyrus the Great, the Emperor, or *Shahanshah* — that is "King of Kings" — liberated the Jews from their "Babylonian Captivity," rebuilt their Temple and was seen as the Great Liberator who was a prefiguration of the Messiah (King) to come.

But the story goes beyond this: Jesus later reconnected with the tradition of the *magi*, became their missionary among his own people and brought the message of the Wise Lord to them in a way many of them could understand. The message of Jesus and the importance of his life, death and resurrection all point in the direction of the faith of Zarathustra. Many of the sayings of Jesus almost exactly parallel material found in the much older sacred languages of the ancient Persian priests. To follow Jesus most perfectly you should not follow the corrupt teachings of institutions founded by those who either did not know him or hated him in life, but rather follow the way that he himself followed— the path of the universal Wise Lord. If you join the Occidental Temple of the Wise Lord, or even just visit us, you can rest assured that you are not breaking any bond with Him, but rather you are seeing things anew with the single eye he always wanted you to see with (Matthew 6.22). Fulfill your faith by believing what He Believed— the universal Truth as revealed by Zarathustra.

There is more about the things that link Jesus and Christianity with the Mazdan Way in a later section.

The Original Green Movement

The contemporary Green Movement can only succeed once a spiritual and intellectual framework has been established which grows from the same roots as does the Green Movement itself. Mainstream Judeo-Christian tradition is well-known to be at the base of many of the negative practices contrary to the Green Philosophy— exploitation of the environment for the exclusive benefit of human-kind. Some Greens have toyed with paganism, but such a path is often arbitrary and without deep conviction. Remarkably the oldest known religion — that is a universal set of beliefs and values not limited to a certain tribe or nation — is an entirely Green form of spirituality: Zoroastrianism. The Occidental Temple of the Wise Lord brings the core essence of the Zoroastrian message to the West in a form we can relate to.

A great thinker, K. Mistree, once wrote that after the Zoroastrian has prepared himself ethically and through other spiritual practices he:

> "... begins to gain an insight into the workings of the physical world. Through this insight an awareness of, and a responsibility towards, the Wise Lord's creations begin to emerge, resulting in a Zoroastrian championing the cause of ecology against those responsible for the pollution and defilement of all that is natural and good in the world. God's world must be kept pure and because of the importance of the general well-being of man in his world, a Zoroastrian is encouraged to live life to its fullest, in order that he may learn to preserve and enjoy the goodness of the seven creations. Monasticism, fasting, celibacy and mortification of the body, are an anathema to a Zoroastrian as it is believed that such practices weaken man and thereby lessen his power to fight evil. Similarly pessimism and despair are sins and in fact are seen as yielding to evil. The task of man is to learn to combat evil with courage, moral fortitude and affirmation."

This ancient faith forms the perfect and natural theoretical model for a true Green spirituality.

Is a Good Religion Even Possible?

It has been said that atheism is the fastest growing "religion" in America today. In a world of scientific advancement and widespread education such a trend is understandable, as religion is seen as a primitive and backward feature of human civilization. Coming of age in Austin Texas in the 1970s and 1980s one could hardly help but be exposed to the ideas of organized atheism, with Madelyn Murray-O'Hare living in your neighborhood.

When one reviews the valid objections conscious atheists have to religion, we who are adherents of the Good Religion, Mazdaism, are glad to see that we would not much raise the ire of the modern atheist.

In fact we could dare to hope to have them see that their objections cannot be to the Good Religion, but only to those who have misused the trappings of religion for destructive purposes. It is our contention that Judaism, Christianity and Islam have all fallen victim to their own propaganda and generated systems destructive to humanity and the planet.

Atheists contend that religious dogma is a limitation on freedom. But Mazdaism does not focus on a system of "thou shalt's" but rather promotes a system of positive and life-affirming and freedom-promoting ideas. Additionally, our first and only prophet, Zarathustra, said that the Wise Lord created mankind to enjoy himself and take pleasure in nature and life.

Atheists argue that religion limits children's rights, which is true when the mainstream religions insist on indoctrinating their children into the dogmas and tenets of their particular sect from the cradle. Mazdans will not initiate a person before their eighteenth birthday. Children must have developed consciousness to the level necessary to make the sacred choice of following the Good Religion, which we call Daena, a word that really means "insight."

The Mazdan Way has been called the "religion of creative evolution." Humanity is *needed* for the Wise Lord's plans to be fulfilled. Man is required to be logical in this world, and also with regard to his explorations of the unknown. From the origin of this religion it has endeavored to remain in accord with scientific thought. Change in theological terms is not a stranger to the Mazdan Way. It is not stagnant or bound by dogmas of the past. This flexibility is achieved by concentrating on certain eternal principles and the direct experience of the power of ancient words.

Critics of church-based religion frequently point to the problem of evil in the world, and logically point out that god cannot be all-powerful, all-good, and all-seeing, otherwise the evil that is patently present in our world could not exist. Churchgoers resort to the phrase "God works in mysterious ways" here. The Wise Lord, as understood in the Mazdan Way, is not yet at full power, and the evil that exists is something that cannot be stopped, except with the evolutionary development of humanity. Mazdans overtly seek to reduce and eliminate all evils, including those caused by organized religion in the past, things such as religiously-based wars and general fanaticism. Mazdan ethics are based on a here-and-now benefit, to one's self as well as to one's fellow human beings, the environment, plants and animals, not to some "suffer now and gain rewards in the hereafter" mentality. This mentality stems from the church's need to coerce the "faithful" into behaviors materially beneficial to the church itself and to its officials.

The Good Religion

The religion of the Wise Lord is known as the *Good* Religion, or even the *Best* Religion. Certainly it is historically the oldest, or first, true universal religion to which any person, regardless of tribal or national affiliation, could *convert* as an act of free choice. This choice must come from good conscience— never as a matter of fear, coercion or force. Because the historical Zoroastrians originally refrained from using any kind of force in their attempts to spread the faith, it did not succeed over time in the way that Christianity and Islam have done. It is now time to renew the world and with it the place of the Mazdan way among the peoples of all the world. The Avestan word for "religion" is *Daena*, which really means "insight." When this insight is gained, one follows the Good as a matter of course, and true conscience, not as a matter of force. The best of us do the Good for the Good's sake alone.

Humans make the choice to follow the Good Religion on a daily basis which mirrors the cosmic choice made in heaven by those yet-unborn souls of humanity at the beginning of the battle. The Wise Lord, in his omniscience, knew that the forces of ignorance and deception — led by the Evil One — would attack the realm of order and truth. This is why God asked the yet-to-be-incarnated souls if they would volunteer to fight in the beautiful material world of his creation on the side of Truth and Order: or *Asha*. A roar went up that echoes through the aeons— and we believe that at that moment each and every human being now living on earth is here as one who made the conscious voluntary choice in heaven to become one of Mazda's soldiers against the Lie. But most humans have forgotten their purpose, their true spiritual heritage and their destiny which is universal salvation and ultimate immortality. This *forgetting* is the result of the effects of the Lie upon us. First you have to awaken to the Truth and to your true nature— then begin in a conscious way to fight for the cause of the Wise Lord. How is this battle fought? This is done through a combination of self-development — awakening true consciousness in your soul — and ethical behavior in the world by practicing the virtues of Good Thoughts, Good Words and Good Deeds.

Many thinking people have wondered how good people from different religions could all be "saved." Each sect and denomination ignorantly believing that those of other sects were inevitably "damned." This idea is wiped away by the Good Religion: Anyone who practices Good Thoughts, Good Words and Good Deeds and whose soul is found to have done more good than bad is in living fact a Mazdan and will as an ordinary course of events, gain a life beyond death and a reward for their goodness. Again, this is the only logical universal answer to the question.

Cosmic Time is divided into three great ages— a time before Good and Evil affected one another, a time in which Evil is attacking and mixing with the Good Creation (this is the time we are in now) and finally one in which Evil will be vanquished and Perfection will reign. The fact that Evil exists — characterized by destructiveness, ignorance, chaos, anger, hate and a myriad of other ugly things — is not denied in the Good Religion. Furthermore, Evil is characterized by one of two traits: excess or deficiency— too much or too little of something. The Good is found in moderation, balance and conscious choices informed by wisdom and insight. God needs humanity to help win the cosmic battle against Evil. God is only able to win in tandem with our efforts. Manifestations of Evil in the world are not the doing of God. Bad things happen to good people because of the activity of Evil. This is never caused by or allowed by God. We must counterattack with Good Thoughts, Good Words and Good Deeds. Because wisdom is superior to ignorance our victory is assured— but we must still fight.

Zarathustra always emphasized that Ahura Mazda wants mankind to *enjoy* life, to grow in knowledge and vital strength, to prosper and feel the pleasures of life. These things, consciously pursued, thwart and combat the Lie.

Historians have pointed out that Zarathustra was:
- The First Prophet of a Universal Monotheistic Religion
- The First Theologian
- The First Philosopher
- The Originator of the Ideas of "Human Rights"
- The First Defender of the Oppressed
- The First Conscious Environmentalist
- The Originator of the Idea of Women's Rights
- The Originator of the Idea of Animal Rights
- The First to Discover the "Power of Positive Thought"
- The Originator of the Practice of Silent Meditation

The Occidental Temple of the Wise Lord is dedicated to conducting this world-struggle by awakening individual souls to their heritage and destiny as well as carrying out ethical and charitable works in the world at large based upon our principles.

Our western branch of the Good Religion is organizationally and culturally independent of the age-old religion of Zoroastrianism, which has been courageously and continually kept alive by followers in India and Iran, and which no longer accepts converts. We maintain our independence out of profound respect for the eastern branch, although we seek to develop and maintain friendly relations with Zoroastrians around the world and acknowledge their wisdom. In this time and age the Wise Lord speaks to us directly to forge a faith for the West inspired by the Zarathustrian vision of the Indo-European pantheon. Our expression takes into account our common roots (our ancient pre-Christian pantheon was similar to that of the ancient Indo-Iranian) and our own Western historical and cultural traditions.

The foundations of the Mazdan Way can be summarized in the following list of teachings:

The Sixteen Guideposts of the Religion (*Daena*)

1. **Ahura Mazda is Consciousness**, pure and abstract wisdom. God's best name is Ahura Mazda, Lord Wisdom, neither male nor female, as *ahura* is masculine and *mazda* was originally feminine.
2. **God is Good**, kind and loving, a friend and leader of humans and all the other gods and goddesses (*yazatas*).
3. **Ahura Mazda is Temporarily *not* Omnipotent**, unable to destroy evil.
4. **Evil exists** as a force contrary to the Good.
5. **The Good is characterized by Balance**, Evil is characterized by Excess and Deficiency.
6. **The Material World is Good**, all Seven Creations were fashioned by Ahura Mazda for the Good and to combat evil.
7. **Spirit and Matter are Equal** in value and are parts of a whole.
8. **God Created Humanity** as a necessary and essential element for World Renovation. Man is Necessary.
9. **All will be Judged.**
10. **All will be Saved**, all humans will achieve salvation. Perfection and life-eternal in perfected form, spiritually and physically, is the destiny of all humans.
11. **Life is to be Enjoyed.**
12. **Good Thoughts, Good Words, Good Deeds** within the framework of the Golden Mean is the essence of the magico-ethical code.
13. **Zarathustra is the only Necessary Prophet.**
14. **The World will be Perfected by God and Man.**
15. **Many Saviors** will aid in the historical development.
16. **The Avestan Texts**, and most especially the Gathas, constitute a magical sound/meaning code, divinely inspired words in which the Truth of Cosmic Order is encoded— the *Râz*.

Practice of the Religion

So many modern religions of the West do not have anything for their believers to *do*. The members of the congregation sit in pews on Sunday and listen to speeches, observe rituals and perhaps do a little sing-along. Otherwise they are merely asked to "have faith" and perhaps occasionally obey a rule or two along the way. Some "study" scripture, but get little understanding from it.

The Mazdan Faith is one of *action*. There is a moment-by-moment engagement in the world and in the spirit. The formula Good Thoughts-Good Words-Good Deeds is far more profound than it seems.

A Mazdan ritually engages in the practice of Good Thoughts through prayerful meditation three to five times a day. He or she learns certain fairly simple rituals to engage in during our numerous celebrations and holidays. One learns to control one's speech and verbal formulations, both as expressed within one's own mind and toward the outside world. This includes the practice of Truth-Telling to combat the force of the Lie wherever it might rear its ugly head. But most importantly the Mazdan manifests Good Action— both by refraining from bad actions and engaging in good ones. These are acts of kindness and aid toward all of the other Creations: the air, water, earth, plants, all beneficial animals, one's fellow man and the ritual Fire. There is an obvious ethical dimension to this and a ritual one. Actively enacting works of worship toward the Wise Lord and the angels (*yazatas*) and celebrations in their honor are *magical* ways to gain much in the realm of Good Deeds. Effective and powerful (i.e. "Good") ritual actions bring one closer to perfection and awareness of and communication with one's Guardian Angel, or the pure spiritual self which eternally remains the bond between you and the world of the gods. A Mazdan is not asked to believe based on no evidence. A Mazdan learns and experiences things which lead to Wisdom and Insight and thus is led to faith by conscience alone.

As you can see we are engaged in a great new adventure. This is a journey of world-transformation. It requires the cooperation of hundreds of talented people in leadership roles. We need artists, philosophers, ritualists, musicians, mystics, astrologers, culinary specialists, architects, linguists, media specialists, designers, fund-raisers, gardeners, pyrotechnicians, IT-specialists, builders, as well as craftsmen and craftswomen of all sorts. But most of all we need men and woman dedicated as warriors for the eternal cause of the Wise Lord.

Our purpose is no small one. We aim to fulfill the ancient prophecies of a light flashing from the east to the West and to introduce a viable form of the Good Religion to Western culture for the first time. Why has it taken so long, in a Western world starved for "something new," for the Mazdan Way to enter our culture in a pure way? The answer can only be that the time was not right until now, and that the Wise Lord simply prevented it from happening until the right time. Now is the time. This book is a sign and your own mission will become clear as you immerse yourself in the history, ideas and practices of the Good Religion. This can be the instrument for the transformation of the world into its final victorious state. Your thoughts, words and deeds from this point forward can bring us all closer to the time of Making-Wonderful.

III. Misconceptions

A great number of misconceptions surrounds the Zoroastrian or Mazdan Way. We should deal with some of these misconceptions early on because they have historically tinged and tainted Westerner's view of Zarathustra and the culture of Iran. Early avoidance of these misconceptions allows for earlier insight. Chief among these is the idea that Zarathustra taught a form of dualism that sets "matter" in opposition to "spirit." This idea, although it does have its origins in Iran, and is dependent on Zarathustran philosophy for its logic, is actually one hundred and eighty degrees opposite from what Zarathustra actually taught. Mazdans have argued against this idea throughout history. In this section we will explore a variety of misconceptions, some great some small. In the process we will further clarify the actual positions of the Mazdan philosophy and theology.

The first question one might ask is: How did so many misconceptions arise? The answer it twofold. First, because so many religions took very fundamental parts of their traditions directly from Zoroastrian teachings and philosophical positions, each of them was often rather anxious to attack the Mazdan tradition as a way to cover their own self-perceived acts of "spiritual theft." But the second answer is the more important one. When Mazdan ideas are communicated from one person to another, or from one people to another, *daevas* of ignorance, deception, fear, anger and all sorts of other disruptive forces are attracted to the channel of communication in order to try to disrupt or jam the frequency of transmission. This is why the sometimes simple, direct and logical ideas of Zarathustra have historically had such a difficult time being heard and understood in their true forms. Misconceptions also arise from various Zoroastrian "heresies" and from historical misunderstandings revolving around the vastness of Iranian spirituality.

Humans often misunderstand things because they tend to measure unfamiliar ideas with tools found in their own cultural patterns and experiences. We tend, for example, to think of a country in older times especially as having one religion. This stems from our limited view of the Christian Middle Ages in Europe. When a country was "Christianized" in the Middle Ages it was officially understood that every subject of a given kingdom was automatically Christian. This was not in fact true, but this is how the cultural myth of the Christian Middle Ages worked. So if we are introduced to a country such as Iran and learn that its religion was Zoroastrianism, we naturally assume that the whole country and everyone in it was a Zoroastrian. Not only was this not true in fact, it was not even something that was believed to be true by the Zoroastrians themselves. For most of the almost four thousand years of history of Zoroastrianism in Iran it has been a minority religion in the country. The peak of its power was in the days of the Sasanian Empire when the majority of the people were professing Zoroastrians or Mazdans. The fact is that the pre-Zoroastrian religion of the Iranians as well as heterodox offshoots of Mazdaism were very common. So the student might meet with Mithraism, for example, and wonder why there is so little of Zoroastrian dualism in it. The reason is because it is a product of pre-Zoroastrian culture. The typical casual student of Mithraism, again by example, will try to project the ideas of Zarathustra into its understanding. This process leads to a misconception, and so it goes.

When a relatively impartial panel of historians of religion and theologians was polled as to what the "best religion in the world" is, Zoroastrianism was the overwhelming answer. If it is the best religion in the history of the world, then why is it not more "popular"? Again the answer probably primarily lies in daevic attack. In another section of this book we will explore more fully what is really meant by "*daeva.*" The answer lies in another misconception of what a "demon" really is.

Dualism

When we speak of dualism we need to understand two different forms: natural and moral. Both of these forms are legitimate and useful to understand. Natural dualism is the logical observation that nature divides things into pairs, day/night, man/woman, up/down, right/left, *ad infinitum*. Besides having certain symbolic or poetic meanings, these dualistic sets are of secondary importance to the great tasks of the religion. The real tension is between the moral precepts of Good and Evil. We have had, and will continue to have, many opportunities to discuss and define the qualities intended by these two words, deeply misunderstood by most people throughout history. The greatest misconception of all is when these moral qualities of Good and Evil are misapplied to spirit (= good) and matter (= evil). This egregious error is the origin of gnosticism. In fact, of course, in the system of Zarathustra "spirit" or the archetypal realm of pre-material prototypes, akin to Platonic *ideas*, are the patterns for the creation of the material universe. This material universe is no less good than the patterns upon which it is based. It is one of the great Lies of the *daevas* that the material universe is "evil" and essentially different from the spiritual realm. This particular Lie, like many of the Lies of Ahriman, act like an addictive drug to the weak and needy minds of the undeveloped and ignorant masses of humanity. This misconception of the good spirit and the evil body is so easy to believe and so simple to conceive of that it seduces the mind quickly. Our hope lies in reversing these trends and educating people to the Truth. Only then will the doors be opened to the progressive evolutionary development of humanity and the material universe. Another way in which Good and Evil are misunderstood by Westerners is because the terms are loaded with Christian connotations. Good being tantamount to obedience and submission to the laws and precepts of the divinity and the church. For the Mazdan it goes well beyond such fairy tale levels of understanding: The Good is that which is intelligent, wise, energetic, independent, joyous, productive and reproductive, efficiently powerful. The Good is what promotes knowledge, power and production, it is beneficial to humanity and to the environment including all of the Creations (Sky, Water, Earth, Plants, Animals, Man and Fire).

Ultimately, Zarathustran dualism can only be fully understood within the context of the doctrine of Ages. In its original and simplest form this was the idea that the ages of the cosmos are three: an Age when Good and Evil are divided one from the other, an Age in which the two are mixed and are in conflict with one another, and finally an Age when Good permanently destroys or limits the effects of Evil and the Good Creation flourishes according to the form in which it was first created. At present we live in the midst of the second of these three Ages. This is only a temporary state of being, which will be transformed at the time of the Making Wonderful.

Zarathustran dualism is eminently logical. It is not the negative and emotion-driven dualism of Manicheanism, rather it is the sober recognition that Evils does make itself felt in this world, and for this there must be a cause. Given the categorical nature of the Wise Lord as something which is entirely Good and Benevolent, this cause cannot lie with God. Its origin is outside God, and its effects on the Seven Creations is is only temporary. However, it is with the cooperation of Man that God will be able to usher in the Third Age and banish the effects of Evil from Creation.

One of the most important things to realize about the relationship between Good and Evil is that the battleground is asymmetrical. The Evil is small and hidden in nooks and crannies everywhere, but it only accounts for a small percentage of the universe. Just as disease-causing bacteria or viruses are only small things in the body of an otherwise healthy person. It does not take much in the way of negative influences to destroy the balance of a healthy organism.

It is also important to remember that the duality exists on the plane of morality not substance. The Good is that which is beneficial and constructive tending toward the improvement and perfection of the

Seven Creations: Sky, Earth, Water, Man, Animals, Plants and Fire. Evil is that which conversely is detrimental and destructive tending toward the detriment and degradation of those same Creations.

It is essential to realize that the Good is not so much a "polar" opposite of Evil, but a radical qualitative difference. Good and evil are not two ends of a spectrum, but two radically different things or qualities. The Good is characterized by the quality of *balance* and moderation, while Evil is marked by extremes bearing the qualities of either deficit or excess— too much or too little of things. Most things can be bad in excess or deficiency, and can be good only in the right balance or right amount. We need water to live, but we can be killed by too much of it at once.

The two different kinds of duality bear more elucidation. As we have noted *natural* duality recognizes the structural and philosophical reality that everything has its opposite. This can be recognized as a proof of the dualistic construct of the world. This structure was intentionally placed in the world as a part of the creative process initiated by Ahura Mazda. *Moral* dualism is an unintended, yet obviously unavoidable, byproduct of creation. It is this moral dualism that is central to the spiritual aspects of work within Mazdan Way. We would not say that night is evil and day good, although we might know that harmful things are more likely to happen at night than in the day. In the Mazdan Way we are more focused on moral dualism: wisdom/ignorance, kindness/cruelty, wealth/poverty. Here we can equate wisdom, knowledge, insight, etc. with the *good* and ignorance, stupidity, shortsightedness, etc. with *evil*. We never want to be ignorant or stupid, that can never be good. Even if we are compelled by circumstances to apply force to solve or rectify a situation, ideally we never want to undertake this act with a cruel heart or do so out of anger. It also goes without saying that we never want to be poor when we could be rich.

In essence the Mazdan Way teaches a polyvalent monotheism: That is there is only one absolute godhead which is the equivalent of the principle of pure focused intelligence or consciousness, however, this creative quality evolved or shaped a multitude of qualities and principles needed to resist and eventually destroy the powers of ignorance, violence and decrepitude which attack the good creation. As such the Mazdan Way is both monotheistic and polytheistic. In historical terms the Prophet Zarathustra had the insight to realize the oneness, goodness and wisdom of the Ahura Mazda, but a wide variety of the old gods and goddesses of the Aryan people remained historically to receive worship and act as coworkers (*hamkāran*) and comrades in the cosmic project.

It might be noted that within the spectrum of Indo-European cultures and mythologies there seems to be an intrinsic model of natural duality. This is especially emphasized in the Iranian, Slavic and Germanic systems, but is also present in the Greek (Olympians : Titans) and Celtic (Tuatha De Danann : Formorians) as well. But it is only with the philosophical insight of Zarathustra that we have the formulas on how to engage in the struggle of good *versus* evil and win.

Heresies

A religion which has been around for almost 4,000 years is bound to have its share of "heretics." A heresy is basically a set of ideas, beliefs or practices which in some major way deviate from a standardized interpretation of doctrine established by an intellectual elite leadership. These ideas may or may not give rise to organizations or popular movements. Given its extreme age, the Good Religion has had far less in the way of heresies than other, much younger religions. But because the Zoroastrian approach to heresy was usually far gentler than other monotheistic organized religious systems, heterodox ideas grew and flourished perhaps to a greater degree than we see elsewhere. These then either passed away into history or had their subtle effects on the established way. Their most lasting impact was not on the religion of Zarathustra, but on other religions such as Christianity which fought them more violently.

The major heretical sects historically linked to the Mazdan religion are Zurvanism and Manicheanism. Iranian ideas are undoubtedly at the deep root of Judeo-Christian Gnosticism, which is one of the major heresies within historical Christianity. Another sort of heresy is presented by the initiatory system of Mithraism which obviously also has its ultimate roots in Iranian tradition. It, however, in no way historically reflected orthodox Mazdan doctrine. Mithraism is not a reaction to Zoroastrian orthodoxy, but is rather a continuation of the older, pre-Zoroastrian mythology.

Some of the so-called heresies of the ancient Mazdan system were actually tolerated and in some cases even encouraged in certain circles in greater Iran throughout its centuries-long history prior to the coming of Islam. It was only during the time of the Sasanian Empire (224-651 CE) that heresies were overtly persecuted. The normal Mazdan response to supposed doctrinal errors is to correct them intellectually and show the practitioner of these erroneous doctrines, the illogic of their ideas, and to demonstrate a better way through good thoughts, good words and good deeds until they come to the conclusion on their own that the true way is the right way. Only when one is convinced internally and by one's own experience that the Mazdan Way is the true way, should one embrace it as the Truth.

Zurvanism

The Zurvanite theology has held a long-standing fascination for scholars of Zoroastrianism. The word *zurvan* simply means "time" in Avestan. It is an abstract concept and appears in the *sih-rozag manthra* for the twenty-first day of the month, which is devoted to Râma Hvâstra and to Vayu. That text reads:

> 21. To Râma Hvâstra; to Vayu, powerful, who defeats the other creatures: to that part of thee, O Vayu, that belongs to Spenta-Mainyu; to the sovereign Sky, to the Boundless Time, to the sovereign time of the long autonomous.
>
> *râmanô hvâštahe vayaoš uparô-kairyehe taraδâtô anyâiš dâmān aêtat tê vayô ýat tê asti spentô-manyaom, θvâšahe hvaδatahe* **zrvânahe** *akaranahe* **zrvânahe** *dareγô-hvaδâtahe.*

It should be noted that this text, where I have set the word for "time" in boldface type, is in Younger Avestan and was composed during the time of the Achaemenid Empire, centuries before there was any Zurvanite cult in Iran.

In many ways Zurvan can be compared to the Germanic concept of Wyrd (ON Urðr). Both have to do with the mysterious effects of time on creation. It could easily be seen that under different circumstances the ancient Germanic peoples might have created a cult of Wyrd to attempt to manipulate the power and effect of time on the lives of individual souls. This is what the cult of Zurvan attempted to do.

It is generally thought that Zurvanism developed as a response to Greco-Roman thought sometime during the Parthian period. The Greeks and Romans were fascinated with astrology and the mechanisms of fate and fortune. Many thinkers in the Classical world believed that a man's destiny was "written" and that his fate was sealed. It was a matter of discovering what that fate was and following it was the revelation of life. Orthodox Mazdans would not agree with this idea: They believed rather that all men were destined for salvation and a Final Body, and that in this life, although the environment may influence events, individual humans were free to make wise choices which would lead to more beneficial outcomes than if the freedom to choose was used to make a bad decision. Although the Iranian magicians were thought by the Greeks and the Romans to be the inventors of "astrology," the way in which this science of the nighttime sky was used by the magi was very different from the way the Greeks and Romans thought it was. The courses of the stars, moon and sun can tell us what challenges we will face, what choices we will be presented with, but these courses do not determine the outcome. That is a matter of will and consciousness. But for a long time period, the Iranians were enamored of the Greco-Roman approach. They did not adopt Greek or Roman solutions, however. Rather they developed a system from within their own mythology: Zurvanism. This sect or philosophical stance grew in Zoroastrian Iran and its own synthesis subsequently informed other sects which spun off from it and spread outside the Iranian sphere of influence

Because Zurvanism was pretty thoroughly eradicated from the ancient Zoroastrian orthodox religion in later Sasanian times, we do not have a great number of documents supporting the beliefs of the sect. But there are some. The most important and detailed ones were composed not by Zurvanites themselves but by Christian opponents of the Persian Zurvanite cult. Just as much of what we know about the Gnostic sects was also actually written by Christian polemicists against the doctrines we are interested in understanding. The fact that we are dependent on this type of source is already discouraging. We cannot be sure of their accuracy. But this evidence combined with what we know from within orthodox Zoroastrianism brings us pretty close to some understanding. The best of these polemics is offered by Eznik of Kolb, a fifth century Armenian cleric who wrote a book *Refutation of the Sects* in which he provides a summary of the Zurvanite beliefs.

> Eznik tells of Zurvan, an apparently hermaphroditic being, whose name means "Time." (Eznik mistranslates it as "Fortune" but we can see why given the context of Iranian interest in Zurvan.) Zurvan sacrifices for a son for a thousand years with no result. Zurvan begins to doubt as to whether all this effort was in vain. At that moment twins were conceived in Zurvan's womb, Ormizd and Ahriman. Zurvan knew that twins were growing in the womb and he vowed that the one that emerged first would be made king. Ormizd heard this and told Ahriman of their father's wish. Once Ahriman heard this he pierced the womb at once to emerge first. He appeared before his father and declared himself his son, but Zurvan did not recognize him: Zurvan said that his son was supposed to be sweet-smelling and radiant, but that this entity was foul-smelling and dark. As they spoke Ormizd emerged, sweet-smelling and radiant. Zurvan at once handed Ormizd a bundle of ritual sticks (the barsom) he used in sacrificing, and told Ormizd that he was his son and that now he was to sacrifice for him just as he had sacrificed for Ormizd. Ahriman objects and holds Zurvan to the vow that was made to make the first-born king. Zurvan acquiesced and appointed a time of 9,000

years in which Ahriman would rule as king under Ormizd's supervision. Zurvan further stipulated to that after this 9,000 year appointed time, Ormizd would be made king to do as he wished. At that point the two brothers began to create and counter-create: "And everything that Ormizd made was good and straight and everything that Ahriman made was evil and crooked."

After giving this account Eznik proceeds to refute the doctrines of Zurvanism as he sees them. Interestingly, these objections are very close to the ones offered by orthodox Mazdans and Zoroastrians against Zurvanism. He says that Zurvan can not be the ultimate god because of the doubts shown, nor can Ormizd (as depicted here) be a wise god, because he shows a lack of foresight by informing Ahriman of Zurvan's intentions, etc. Eznik goes on to criticize belief in astrology, etc. as these were important parts of Zurvanite and Greco-Roman thought of the day. In all of this he is correct. Of course, if he was an orthodox Christian he would have to explain why his own god is shown to be a jealous, wrathful and fearful figure— neither traits becoming an absolute deity. Eznik's own Armenian Christianity was probably heavily influenced by orthodox Zoroastrian philosophical ideas regarding the character of deity.

If we put the Zurvanite theology into a schematic diagram it would appear something like this:

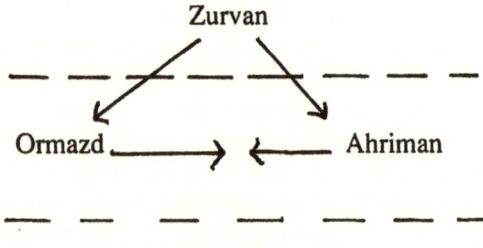

In the philosophically grounded doctrine of actual Zarathushtran theology Ahura Mazda (Ohrmazd) and Angra Mainyu (Ahriman) have different origins, they both come from the void (Pah. *tuhīgīh*), but Ahura Mazda is positive, complete and radiant with light, whereas Angra Mainyu is negative, broken, and a shadow of reality. Simply put, since we can all see that things such as ignorance, weakness, poverty all exist, and know that they cannot be ascribed to the divinity, they must have another origin, i.e. the *daevas*. This is more a matter of logic and philosophy than it is mythology.

The more usual representation of the scheme above would be:

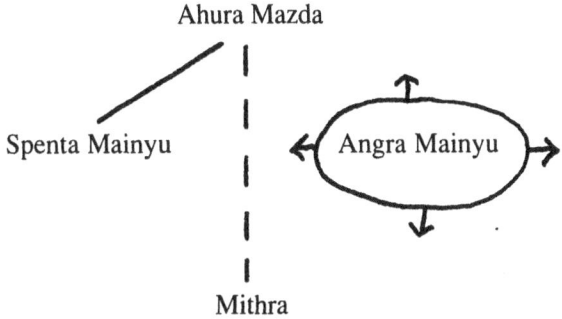

This shows that although Ahura Mazda did not create Angra Mainyu (Ahriman), this entity does form an opposite force to the *yazatas*, at the head of which can be seen Spenta Mainyu (Holy Mentality/Spirit). The true meaning of Angra Mainyu is "Destructive Mentality." Mithra is always seen as the intercessor between humanity and the *yazatas*.

Although Zurvanism has fascinated Western scholars, as a matter of fact the true nature of the sect remains unknown. It may have just been an erroneous interpretation of Mazdan theology favored by a group of Magian priests, or it may have been a dominant alternative to mainstream Mazdan theology and philosophy which held sway for a time in the Sasanian period.

If we return to the interpretation of the *sirozah* quoted at the beginning of this section we will learn some interesting points about Zurvan and its position in the Mazdan Way. The manthra is devoted to both Râman a giver of joy, peace and security, and who also provides for fertile fields and healthy plants. But mostly it is dedicated to the ancient *yazata* known as Vayu. Vayu is originally an extremely archaic Indo-European deity of the *atmosphere*. This is the space between the surface of the earth and the vault of heaven or celestial sphere. Within this space move all of the planets and the sun and moon. It is said that even Ahura Mazda enlisted the aid of Vayu in order to strike against Angra Mainyu. It is within the space defined by Vayu that the battle between Good and Evil occurs. This results in the mixture of Good and Evil within Vayu, so that it can be said that there are beneficent and malevolent aspects to Vayu.

> There is a sense of the "neutrality" of Vayu, for there is both a good and an evil Vayu. Some scholars believe that in later thought he was divided into two figures, but in the early period there was the idea of one figure embodying the dual features of a beneficent yet sinister, awesome power, the pitiless one who is associated with death, whose paths no one can escape. If properly propitiated he will deliver men from all assaults, for the wind moves through both worlds, the world of the Good Spirit and the world of the Evil Spirit. He is the worker of good, the destroyer, the one who unites, the one who separates.
>
> (Hinnells 1973, p. 31)

It is telling that *zurvan*, "time." is mentioned in the context of Vayu in both its *boundless* and *finite* forms as the matrix in which Vayu works, for both good and ill. It is from this mechanism and mythic paradigm that the sect of Zurvanism seems to have drawn its inspiration.

Many reading these words will have been struck by the similarity between Vayu and the Germanic god Wôðanaz. Most of this is the result of a common genetic link from within the Indo-European paradigm, but it is not beyond question that the connections between Vayu and Vāta in the Iranian pantheon and Wôðanaz in the Germanic one are the result of various times in which Iranian systems and the world of Germanic mythology were in special contact: from the age of the Germanic ethnogenesis (ca. 700 BCE) to the mission of Armenian bishops to Iceland in the eleventh century.

In the final analysis the doctrine of Zurvanism is an erroneous belief system because it limits the intellect and freedom of Man by binding him to ideas of fate and material motions of natural objects. It also limits the nature and majesty of the divinity itself, Ahura Mazda, by making this divinity derivative of, and dependent on, a prior being, Time or Zurvan. In fact Zurvan is a mechanism created and employed by Ahura Mazda to give shape and direction to Creation and also to ensnare Angra Mainyu that he might be defeated and eliminated at the end of the appointed time span. It is probably most likely that the cult of Zurvanism was the result of Greco-Roman influence on the philosophy of the Iranians. The Greeks and Romans typically believed in the power of Fate and the compelling force of the motion of the planets (which they identified with their gods) on the life of humans. Zoroastrian astrology, on the other hand, was a tool for the prediction of possibilities and openings for opportunities for the application of human or divine will in order to alter events in the material world (*getig*).

The great and influential scholar of Zoroastrianism R. C. Zaehner was heavily criticized by the Zoroastrian faithful for his misinterpretation of the primacy of the Zurvanic myth. Clearly

Zurvanism is an attractive myth because it is so dramatic and stark in its presentation: Time giving rise to two twin brothers, one good one evil who engage in a cosmic battle for dominion of the world. But it is philosophically untenable, and it holds no special place for humanity, as does the Mazdan philosophy. Zurvanism had more effect on cults outside Zoroastrianism than it did within the religion itself. Once when I asked a Zoroastrian student of mine about Zurvan, he looked puzzled and said that he thought Zurvan might be some sort of "demon."

Gnosticism

Gnosticism was the most important Christian heresy in the early history of that religion. Without Zoroastrian doctrines of dualism it is doubtful whether Gnosticism would have had a basis for its teachings. Gnosticism is essentially a twisting of Zoroastrian doctrines into the opposite of its original meaning. There is no firm source material for the history of Gnosticism before the first or second century CE. It appears to be a Judeo-Christian misreading and misinterpretation of Zoroastrian ideas fashioned to negate the importance of the material world and in fact relegate it to the status of an evil creation of an evil god. In other words it is a world-denying religion. Its history is ultimately rooted in Zoroastrianism, and more directly in Platonism. Zoroastrian philosophy holds that Good and Evil are moral concepts, that there is a Good and Evil Mentality opposed to one another, but that the material universe is by and large a good creation, mixed with pollution created by the Evil Mentality. The individual human being has the choice every moment of every day to choose either good or bad thoughts, words and deeds. Plato's views were also largely pro-cosmic, that is he saw the material world as generally good, but less good than the mental or spiritual realm. Zoroastrians see equal goodness in all levels. So Plato opened the door and suggested the relative evil of the material world, he called the body the "dungeon of the soul" and likened the world to a prison from which the soul yearned to escape.

It must be said that this trait of being a world-denying or world-rejecting religion is not limited to Gnosticism. This same tendency is found in Hinduism and Buddhism in the East. Originally the Vedic Religion in India was world-affirming, but in the transition into what came to be called Hinduism the world became a place of sorrow (*samsara*) and a place the soul yearned to escape from. More radically, the Buddha claimed that the self, the soul and the world itself did not even exist! It is found that such "solutions" to spiritual problems often lead to more failure than success in the practical world.

The whole subject of Gnosticism is too complex to enter into here, and it is not the purpose of this essay to explain all of its intricacies, but rather to focus on it as a misrepresentation of Mazdan ideas. For anyone interested in delving into this topic further there are a number of good introductions, such as the ones by Rudolph, Jonas and Walker.

Gnosticism has its own literature, most of which was destroyed by orthodox Christian zealots, but some of which survives. The most significant body of writing is found in the famous Nag Hammadi Library— a find of Coptic texts made in the Egyptian desert in the late 1940s. Prior to this there were a few important Gnostic books such as the *Pistis Sophia* and the *Book of Jeu* as well as an array of quotes from Gnostic teachings made by Christian polemicists in their attacks on Gnosticism.

The Gnostics had their own interpretations of canonical texts of the Judeo-Christian tradition. In other words, a Gnostic would read a biblical passage with totally different eyes than the orthodox Christian. Many of these readings betray a Mazdan or Zoroastrian attitude, even if the symbols often seem aberrant. An example of this can be found in the Old Testament Book of Genesis. This book was actually composed during a time when the Jews were heavily influenced by Persian ideas. This was the time of their so-called Babylonian Captivity. The major constellation of iconic symbols found in the text are of Iranian origin: a garden, the first man and woman, sacred tree(s), a serpent, etc. The story goes that a god created the first man and woman and placed them in a garden which contained two trees, an outer one the fruit of which could provide knowledge of good and evil and an inner one the fruit of which could provide immortality (i.e. the tree of life). This god told the innocent creatures, Adam and Eve, man and woman, that they could eat of any tree in the garden, but commanded them not to eat from these two. One day the woman was tempted by a serpent in the tree of the Knowledge of Good and Evil to eat of its fruit and she and the man, Adam, ate from it and then knew good and evil, i.e. they became human with awareness of right and wrong, this and that, etc. The god that had created them became angry at their disobedience and drove them out of the Garden of Eden cursing them with mortality, cursing the woman with the pain of childbirth. In the text of Genesis (3) it is reported that god says to the angels: "Behold, the man is become as one of us, to know good and evil; and now lest he put forth his hand, and take also of the tree of life, and eat, and live for ever." Here the god betrays his fear and anger for man's disobedience. Theologians tell us that the reason god created man was to have someone to love and praise him of his own free will, and that when man disobeyed, god reacted by cursing man and woman and driving them away. Now a Zoroastrian would look at this story from a different angle: The god who claims to be the creator cannot be such. The creator of humanity loves humanity and needs humanity to complete the plan to eradicate evil in the cosmos. God (the Wise Lord) wants man to have knowledge, and man is already blessed with a future immortality. So the Mazdan god only wants for man what the god of the Old Testament wants to prevent man from having: knowledge and immortality. The Old Testament "god" appears to Mazdan eyes to be a *daeva*: jealous, wrathful, fearful and petulant, desiring praise and blind obedience without informing his creatures so they can understand the reason for his commands. (Of course if they are kept in ignorance they cannot understand the reasons anyway.) In this narrative the serpent appears as the hero and representative of the true god of light and knowledge (*gnosis*). Ahura Mazda is a friend and mentor. The Wise Lord wants us to develop knowledge, realize who and what we are — divine beings (*fravashis*) — who have volunteered to be born into this world to be the comrade and coworker of god in the struggle to eradicate evil and promote the good. The Old Testament god wants man to be passive, obedient, ignorant, as if a child. Ahura Mazda wants mankind to grow up, develop, take up positions in the ranks of the armies of the good to fight the minions of Angra Mainyu and defeat the forces of ignorance, violence and poverty by becoming wise, kind and powerful.

The idea of man having a choice between good and evil is originally an Iranian idea. But the Jews (and subsequently the Christians) made this a one-time choice made by the original man (Adam), who, through fault that is entirely his own, supposedly chose wrong and now all men suffer the eternal negative consequences of his choice. (The whole story reads like a Kafka novel when you boil it down to its constituent parts.) In the Iranian version man is a volunteer force for good in this world, but man is attacked on all sides by negative impulses and mentalities sent to him by the *daevas* who wish only to prevent individuals from awakening to their true natures and heritage in order to defend themselves from their ultimate defeat. Man is not at fault for his situation and will be rewarded for his brave act of voluntary service in the world with ultimate perfection and immortality. Man is, however, responsible for awakening and discovering the Truth, making the right choice every moment of every day as a warrior for the Wise Lord. These are two radically different views of god, two radically different views of humanity. It is clear where each road leads.

In a very real sense it can be said that the Mazdan Way is a humanistic way. The Judeo-Christian view of man is that his nature is that of a damned sinner, un-needed by god, whose only salvation comes through the unearned *grace* of god. The Mazdan view is humanistic, but not merely the humanism of the secular ideologues of recent times: so-called secular humanism. Rather it is the great humanism of the Renaissance, a humanism that is *both* secular and celestial— both equally.

The Gnostic view is vigorously rejected by the Mazdan thinker. This is because the Gnostic sees the natural universe as a horrible place and the body as something to be escaped. The Mazdan sees both the supernal realm of *menog* and the manifest world of *getig* as equally good, it is just that getig has been severely polluted by the forces of the *daevas*. The bad that occurs in this world is not because the world is bad, but rather because bad patterns of thought, bad paradigms of action have asserted themselves in our world and in our lives.

Manicheanism

By far the most successful sub-branch of the Gnostic tradition is Manicheanism. This is one of the world's first religions created by a single individual as a virtual work of art. Its roots in the Iranian world are multifaceted, both indirect and direct. The founder and prophet of the religion, Mani (216-276 CE) was brought up among the Elchasaites, a Parthian baptist sect of Judeo-Christianity founded just over a hundred years before Mani's birth located in Mesopotamia. This community is likely linked to the Qumran sect responsible for the so-called Dead Sea Scrolls. Mani was born into an aristocratic Parthian family, but his upbringing was entirely within the community of this sect. He was sickly from birth and probably lame as an adult. At the ages of twelve and twenty-four he received revelations. The latter of these was from an angel acting as a messenger for the King of the Paradise of Lights— the supreme god of his system. This supreme deity is also sometimes referred to by the name Zurvan. The message commanded him to leave the sect and proclaim his own revelation.

Mani first traveled to the East, where at Sind in northwestern India he converted a Buddhist ruler. Then he went to Iran where he gains the support of the Emperor, Shapur I. He is given permission to preach his doctrine throughout the Empire. The prophet had great success in his lifetime and founded many churches and monasteries in various lands along the Silk Road.

Zoroastrianism was already, and for the first time in history, the official *state religion* of the Sasanian Empire. The fact that Mani was allowed to spread his system is a testimony to Persian tolerance on the one hand, but also to the idea that the truth of Zarathustra must be realized in each individual heart based on conscience— not coercion by the state or any authority. Differing ideas were allowed to be expressed.

Mani's sect spread like wildfire in the Empire and drew the ire of the chief Zoroastrian priest, Kerdir. After the death of the *Shahanshah*, Shapur I a subsequent emperor, Bahram I, was persuaded by Kerdir to shun and imprison Mani. After twenty-six days the founder of Manicheanism died in prison at the age of sixty, probably due to the conditions under which he was constrained. He was not actively killed or executed.

The religion founded and promoted by Mani would remain an influential ideology for a thousand years. It not only survived that long in regions stretching from China to Europe it also caused its many opponents to have to address the issues raised by Mani's philosophy. It was vigorously attacked by Christians, and Muslims, as well as Neoplatonist philosophers and even Zoroastrians themselves. For Christians the opposition was fierce— Manicheanism was considered **the** heresy *par excellence*. This is perhaps because the "cultural DNA" of Manicheanism and Christianity were so close. The "real founding father" of Christianity as an ideology was Augustine of Hippo (354-430) who spent ten years of his life as a practicing Manichean before converting to Christianity. Although Christianity as a theological construct took great pains to distinguish itself from Mani's approach, the underlying attitudes of Manicheanism seem to have penetrated the Christian soul. Mani's model of the spirit being good and all matter evil, his disgust for the human body and sexuality as well as his celibacy, all strike the casual observer as being very "Christian." Of course, the Christian theologian will counter that Christian doctrine is totally different, yet anyone who has experienced a real-life culture generated under strong Christian social dominance will beg to differ.

It is a general good rule of thumb when considering the history of Christian ideas that if a feature of thought or practice found in Christianity does not have its root cause in Judaism, the cause is to be sought elsewhere. Huge amounts of later Christian practice is to be discovered in the pagan cultures which were absorbed by the Church. However, these anti-material, anti-physical, and anti-sexual ideas cannot have their roots in Greek, Roman or Germanic paganism! And again, in the actual experience of Christianity, nothing seems more correct than to insist that the spirit is good and the flesh is evil, heaven is good and the world is evil... This betrays the enormous impact of the erroneous teaching of Mani and is the best explanation for why the Zoroastrian priests felt he had to be stopped.

While Christian thinkers spent volumes attacking Manicheans and their many offshoot sects (Bogomils, Cathars, Waldensians) the Zoroastrians simply stated the errors of Mani and left it at that.

It is remarkable that Mani consciously set out to create a new religion taking bits and pieces from other religions he had studied. From the Zoroastrians he took truth-telling, the symbolism of light and the hierarchization of the cosmos. From the Buddhists he adopted the concept of non-injury to others and reincarnation. From the Christians he acquired his ascetic attitude (self-denial) and the important "myth of Christ."

Mani adopted a conscious chameleon strategy for the spread of his church and his system continued to thrive in this vein after his death. It had success all along the Silk Road and briefly became the state religion of the Uighur Turks in Central Asia (763-840). However, in general Manicheans remained a distrusted minority. Sometimes they became secretive, claiming in public to be orthodox Christians, Muslims, Buddhists, Taoists, etc.

Basically Mani taught that the spiritual light was trapped in matter and that for the Manicheans the purpose of human life was "to strive actively to liberate particles of light through their rituals and practices." (Foltz 2004, p. 107) One of the main ways imprisoned light was liberated in the world was by the consumption of raw, uncooked food in a ritual setting with the subsequent singing of hymns designed to send the light liberated from their veggies soaring heavenward on the wings of song.

Among the errors of Manicheanism pointed out in the Zoroastrian book *Denkard* are: The claim that humans were by nature bad, when in fact they are good; that the world and matter are bad, when they are likewise good; that the world and man were created by a demonic entity, when in fact they were created by the Wise Lord. Other errors include that agriculture is light-destroying, when in fact it is a good endeavor to grow crops, that the world is filled with demons that need to be expelled, while the Zoroastrian sees a world mainly filled with angelic beings to be drawn close to man. Also, the Manichean obsession with celibacy is an anathema to the Mazdan who sees the procreation of humanity and the pleasures of sexuality as good things provided to man by the Wise Lord.

We can perhaps admire Mani for his brilliance, creativity and determination, but it is useless to delve any further into his teachings, as they are fundamentally flawed due to the erroneous premises concerning the very natures of the world, man and God.

Although it is true that Mani's death was obviously caused by the conditions of his incarceration, the general tolerance extended to him and his church is really what is astounding. That he was freely allowed to teach his anti-world, anti-human and anti-nature system in a culture that so much valued these Creations is remarkable.

The clearest way to look at the error of Mani is that his system teaches that the world is a bad place and that it is man's task to try to *escape* it. Eliade concludes that Manicheanism "consists in escaping from the prison built by demonic forces and in contributing to the definitive annihilation of the world, life, and of man." (HRI, II, p. 394) The Mazdan sees a world much beset and under attack by evil forces, but it is a battlefield and a workshop— it is man's job in tandem with the Wise Lord to win the battle and perfect the divine product. To want to escape the field of battle is to have the soul of a coward and deserter! In the midst of the battle, as the din becomes great and the blood begins to fly, the Manichean seeks to run, while the Mazdan hearkens to the orders from the Lord and turns his shoulders into the fight.

Although Manicheanism is for all intents and purposes dead, its pattern can sometimes still be seen in movements which glumly preach the expendability of humanity and human life, along with strains of asceticism and puritanism. It left its indelible mark and stain on Christianity, despite the vicious attacks by the Church, in some respects Christian culture can be seen to imitate many of Mani's attitudes on the popular level. This is because the most important Christian philosopher, Augustine of Hippo, was himself originally a Manichean.

Mithraism

Mithraism cannot be called a Zoroastrian heresy *per se* in that it was most likely a survival of pre-Zoroastrian tradition that was exported from the Iranian world into the West in a particular form. As an ideology it does not attempt to criticize or deal with orthodox Zoroastrian ideas or problems. It has its own set of ideas and traditions rooted in the same soil as orthodox Zoroastrianism, but with entirely different branches.

For an in-depth look at some of the possible symbolic teachings connected with Mithraism of the Hellenistic time period just before the inception of Roman Mithraism, see my book *The Magian Tarok* (Lodestar [originally 2006]).

History

The history of Mithraism is complex and often controversial. Early scholars such as Franz Cumont looked at the evidence and made the logical conclusion that it was, as it obviously appears to be, an import from the Iranian world adopted by the Romans and made their own. As the scholarly pendulum swung, as it is wont to do, later scholars concluded that Mithraism was an entirely Roman creation based on superficial Iranian symbols in the spirit of Ivy League frat-boys using American Indian symbols to dress up their farcical rites. As scholars have also begun to look at Mithraism from the Iranian side as well, it appears that the real answer is somewhere in the middle.

It seems most reasonable to conclude that the Mysteries of Mithra were developed and evolved a particular form in the period of the Parthian Empire (247 BCE - 224 CE) within the borders of that empire. It should be remembered that this empire followed on the domination of Iran by the Macedonians during the time following the conquest of the Achaemenid Empire by Alexander (331 BCE). For these centuries there was a mixture of Greek and Iranian ideas, especially among the population not a part of the orthodox Zoroastrian priesthood. This latter group held itself aloof from Greek influence, but clearly the Mithraic cult was something that was developed outside the orthodox religion. Among the Romans it became a framework in which all of the esoteric teachings of the East, including Persian religion in its various forms, astrology, numerology, etc., could be synthesized and brought into an initiatory context.

We know that there was a strong cult of Mithras in the regions of Armenia, Cappadocia (in central Asia Minor), Pontos (northern Asia Minor), and among a group of pirates who had bases in southern Asia Minor. This cult was connected to that of the ancient Persian god Mithra, but was evolving into something different in many respects.

Armenia had been part of the Persian Empire off and on for centuries. Many Zoroastrian fire temples were built there, and there were obviously many temples built to Mithra there as well. This was so prevalent that the Armenian word for Mithra-temple (*mehean*) became the word for "temple" in general. We know that the Mysteries of Mithras seem to have originated in Italy and to have quickly spread north from there. Many have expected to find this cult to have entered from the eastern provinces of the empire and spread westward. It is most likely that the point of entry into the Roman Empire came in 66 CE when Tiridates the Persian king of Armenia, who was a Zoroastrian priest and founder of the Arsicid Dynasty among the Parthians, came to Rome to be crowned king of Armenia by the Roman Emperor Nero. This marked peace with the Parthians and ceding of the Armenian region to the Persians. Franz Cumont was the first to speculate that it was from this connection with the City of Rome and the Zoroastrian religion that the cult of Mithras originated. Subsequent scholars have rejected this idea, yet it seems to fit the facts quite well. Those who insist on calling the Mysteries of Mithra a *Roman* cult, invented for and by Romans, miss the large point that almost nothing of the Mithraic mythology is explicable or clarified by Roman myth, whereas Persian mythic iconography and religious doctrines often shed vast amounts of light on Mithraic evidence.

Although orthodox Zoroastrians may have been connected to Mithra-worship in Armenia and elsewhere in the Parthian Empire, it must generally be said that the cult of Mithra even among the Iranians appears to be an example of the continuation of the worship of the old gods from the pre-Zoroastrian system. We know that this "Iranian paganism" continued to exist side by side with orthodox Zoroastrianism in the Persian Empire throughout its history. Apparently many scholars have the mistaken idea that pre-Zoroastrian religion somehow ceased with the acceptance of the Prophet's religion by the imperial court. With the realization that these old cults continued to exist, many things that may not have made sense to those who want to see in Mithraism a reflection of pure orthodox Zoroastrian ideas will suddenly make more sense. Orthodox Zoroastrianism tended to be very tolerant of unusual beliefs, witness Manicheanism and Zurvanism, in the core belief that people should come to understand the logic and truth of Zarathustra's system as a matter of conscience, not coercion.

One of the astounding facts about Mithraism is that it left us at least 420 extant archeological sites called Mithraea: subterranean spaces in which the rites were performed. These have tended to survive because they were underground and after they were closed they lay forgotten until they were discovered later, often by accident. There must have been hundreds more of these in history and it has been estimated that there were as many as 600 Mithraea in the City of Rome itself. One of these is under the Vatican. Both the great number of these sites and their elaborate nature indicate to us just how widespread and important this cult was in the Roman Empire.

Men — and only men could be initiated into the mysteries of Mithras — from many different nations and tribes joined the Roman army during this period. A great many of them were from Germania and it is along the German limes or borderlands between the Roman Empire and Free Germany that a great number of Mithraea are found. It has been widely assumed that some men took Mithraic concepts away with them and brought them back into their native tribal cults when and if they returned home after their service to Rome had ended. Contemporary scholars have compared Mithras to Wodan and to the Norse figure Heimdallr.

What brought the Mysteries of Mithras to an end? Like all things that are defeated in history, it was a combination of a vicious enemy and unpreparedness on the part of the Mithrists. They faced off with the Christians who both engineered the fall of the Roman Empire and subverted it in order to establish their religion as the only acceptable religion in what remained of the empire. By 400 CE no Mithraeum was active. Pagan critics of Christianity pointed out that it was essentially a criminal gang made up originally of slaves, servants, shady characters and foreigners. The Mithraic cult was loyal to the empire, to the emperor and to the traditions of Rome, even if the origin of the cult was a foreign one itself. The violence with which Mithric art and property was destroyed, the mass killing of Mithric loyalists all point to the violent end of the Mysteries of Mithras in Rome.

Theory and Theology

Because Mithraism has left no canonical texts behind, if there ever were any, it is very difficult to know with any great precision what the Mithrists believed or taught. We are dependent on what was said *about* them, analysis of the archeological remains and the inscriptions found in the Mithraea, of which there are approximately one thousand. These inscriptions are mostly dedicatory formulas telling us that so-and-so paid for this or that feature in the Mithraeum. The importance of these lies in the fact that it shows that men of all professions and backgrounds were important in the cult. Scholarly work on Mithraism has been quite intense over the past several decades resulting in our being able to be fairly certain about the content of the teachings of the cult of Mithras. The history of how these beliefs and rituals originated and by what means they were transported into the Roman Empire seem to be the most controversial aspects of Mithraic studies at this juncture.

The Mithrists had a good reputation for being moral and ethical in their dealings with one another and with their fellow citizens. This angered the Christians who accused the Mithrists of "imitating" Christian teachings and rituals. In fact, of course, all of the things they accused the Mithrists of were merely those teachings and practices which both had inherited from Mazdan practice and ethics. The practice of the eucharist, i.e. the consecrating of bread and water or wine to be consumed by the worshipper in ritual was an ancient practice of the Persians. This is fundamental to the *yasna* ritual. Mithrists engaged in sacral meals or banquets in their ceremonies, and, of course, the Christians have their highly symbolic (and stingy) eucharist ritual. None of this appears to come form Judaic or Roman practice *per se*, but rather is a *magical* ritual borrowed from the Persians.

It may well be that the cult of Mithras was keyed to the Persian Zurvanite ideology. This would fit insofar as the Mithraic ideology was certainly bound to astrological teachings and purposes and Zurvan, as Time, was the integral concept in this ideology. Zurvan is identified as both Greek Aion and Kronos, Roman Saturn, and the degree of Saturn is the highest initiatory degree in the Mithraic Mysteries. Saturn governs the zone just on this side of the vault of the night-time sky. A numerological link between Mithras and Saturn is shown here using the Greek spelling of the name of Mithras:

$$\mu = 40$$
$$\epsilon = 5$$
$$\iota = 10$$
$$\theta = 9$$
$$\rho = 100$$
$$\alpha = 1$$
$$\sigma = 200$$

Μειθρας = 365

Mithras was a cosmic god who mastered time and space and who had the power to intercede on the initiate's behalf to protect him, cause him to succeed and ultimately to transport his soul to the realm of the stars while he still lived.

Myth

Mithras is said to have been born in a cave made of rock on December 25. The significance of this lore is as follows: Mithras is the light, the light of the stars. In the archaic mythology of the Iranians the vault of heaven, the dome of the sky, is seen to be made of rock crystal. Thus the space between the earth and the vault of heaven is like an enormous cosmic *cave*. Mithras is born out of the rock as the starlight penetrates the rock from above. This event occurred around the winter solstice. Clearly the early Christians "borrowed" some of this symbolism (savior born on December 25 in a cave) in order to compete with Mithraism in the war of religions that was taking place in the waning years of the Roman Empire.

The reason why virtually no Mithraea have been found in Iran is that there the cult was held in actual natural caves and caverns. The Roman soldiers were usually trained civil engineers and could readily build small artificial caverns, even in urban settings, to suit their needs.

Certain features of Mithraic mythology correspond in an interesting way with Mazdan mythology. Mithras becomes a sun-god among the Romans, whereas Mithra is a god of light (of the dawn or of the stars) in Iran. In Iran Mithra is a protector of the cattle, whereas in Rome he is seen as a cattle rustler and cattle-killer. This certainly can be explained as a reflection of the older, pre-Zoroastrian view of the god Mithra. The killing and/or sacrifice of a bovine signals radical cosmic change in Iranian myth. Angra Mainyu conspires to cause the death of the original cosmic bovine (Gavaevodata), from whose purified seed all animals are generated by Ahura Mazda. The tauroctony, or bull-killing icon, of the Roman Mithrists certainly alludes to some of these ideas. We see that a ear of wheat is emerging from the bull, and that an evil creature (a scorpion) is trying to attack the source of the bull's seed, his testicles. All of these motifs seem to refer to the same mythic paradigms as the Iranian material. Another, and perhaps more to the point, example of the sacrifice of a bull leading to world change is found in the *Bundahishn* (30, 25), where we read that the final *saoshyant*, or "savior," will sacrifice a bull and in connection with this prepare the final *haoma*— the sacred drink which will result in the manifestation of man's Final Body in which all humans will attain immortality in a physical sense. So the bull-sacrifice is intimately connected to world-change, human perfection and immortality. As we will see, these ideas are very ancient in Zoroastrianism, and were taken into Christianity in imitation of these archaic Persian doctrines.

The particular myth of Mithras of the mysteries was reconstructed by Cumont (*Mysteries*, pp. 132-138) as follows:
> One day Mithras attempted to capture the cosmic bull, which was grazing in the mountains. The divine hero jumped on the bull's back and seized him by the horns although the bull was able to throw Mithras off, the hero never let go of the horns. He was thus dragged along the ground, where he suffered terribly— but he never released the horns. Eventually the bull was exhausted and Mithras dragged him by the hind feet to his home, which was in a cave. (The dragging of Mithras was called the *transitus*, and is a symbol of man's sufferings.)

The bull, however, succeeded in escaping from the cave and again roamed in the mountains. The divinity of the Sun sent his messenger, the raven, to Mithras to tell him to slay the bull. Mithras did not want to do this deed, but was commanded to do so by the Solar deity, and so he obeyed. He set out to hunt the beast with his trusty dog. They hunted the cosmic bull back to the cave, where Mithras was able to deliver a deadly blow to the back of the animal with his knife. This is the scene, of the *tauroktonia* (bull-slaying), is displayed in the apse of virtually every Mithraeum.

From the spinal column of the bull sprang wheat (source of man's daily bread and that which is sacrificed in the Mysteries), from his blood sprang the vine (source of the sacred drink of the Mysteries) and from his seed (which was purified by the Moon, see *Bundahishn*, ch. X) sprang all beneficial animals. Thus Mithras facilitated the creation of the world as we know it.

Another important cosmological function of Mithras involves his chariot, or quadriga, pulled by four cosmic horses. They circumscribe the pole in the north. The outermost horse is fiery and moves with great velocity around the pole, the next (airy) one moves slower and the next (watery) one slower still, finally the innermost (earthy) horse stands in one place and turns at the pole. The fire of the breath of the first horse ignites the mane of the innermost horse and the four are transformed into a single quintessential whole. (See Cumont *Mysteries*, pp. 116-118.)

Ritual and Initiation

The Mithraeum is a venue or theater for the performance of the rituals of Mithraism. It was built and designed specifically for this purpose. By contrast, although Christian churches *became* this over time, originally they had no special design features beyond what was seen in the main hall of a home of an affluent Roman of the day.

We know that there were elaborate rituals of initiation and seasonal celebration carried out in the Mithraea. What the exact liturgy was is a matter of reconstruction. The famous "Mithras Liturgy" (PGM IV.475-829) may, or may not, be of a great deal of help.

Mithraism was a religion with a number of initiatory degrees. Each of these endowed the initiate with greater power and blessings:

Servitors:	1. Corax = Crow or Raven	= Mercury
	2. Cryphius = Occult	
	(or Nymphus = Groom)	= Venus
	3. Miles = Soldier	= Mars
Participants:	4. Leo = Lion	= Jupiter
	5. Mithra = Mithras	
	(or Perses = the Persian)	= Luna
	6. Heliodromus = Courier of the Sun	= Sol
	7. Pater = Father	= Saturn

In general the initiatory degrees describe an ascension of the soul from the earth to the highest sphere of Saturn at the border or edge of the cosmos. It is noteworthy that the course of the soul does not follow the natural order of the planetary spheres (as they were envisioned by the scientific theories of the day). That order was: Moon-Mercury-Venus-Sun-Mars-Jupiter-Saturn. The priestly Mithraic initiate would undergo the following transformations at the various degree levels:

Corax/Mercury: Base desire abandoned, noble desires perfected.
Nymphus/Venus: Harmful appetites purified into an appetite for truth.
Miles/Mars: Anger and irrational violence abandoned and a mantel of courage assumed.
Leo/Jupiter: Illusory dreams given up and replaced by a sublime determination and will.
Mithras/Moon: Old vital and nutritive energies are relinquished and replaced by immortal energies.
Heliodromus/Sun: False doctrines and ideas are rejected for a pure and direct intellective faculty.
Pater/Saturn: Entry into the gate of the stars.

This profound system of initiatory self-transformation demonstrates a deep understanding of the doctrines of Mazdan astrology, which considered the planetary spheres to be fraught with *daevic* qualities, damaging the soul in negative ways as it descends into incarnation from above. The Mithraic formula of initiation systematically purifies the candidate of these negative traits and replaces them, or transforms them into positive ones.

Iconography

Certainly the most conspicuous single feature of Mithraic evidence is the iconography of the tauroctony: the bull-slaying scene. There are hundreds of examples of this scene in the archeological record. No two are exactly the same, but all contain the following elements: Mithras stabbing the bull in the shoulder with a knife or dagger, while holding the bull's snout and looking away from the scene, ears of wheat sprout from the bull's tail and/or blood, there is a dog lapping at the blood, a snake either also drinking the blood or attempting to do so (the dog occasionally prevents this), a scorpion attacks the bull's genitalia, and there are two torchbearers in the scene, one holds his torch upward, the other holds his downward.

The Tauroctony

What does this all mean? There are various interpretations. Again there are no Mithraic books which lay out the meaning of the iconography from ancient times. Some identify the figures with constellations or stars, e.g. the snake with Draco, the scorpion with Scorpio the dog with Canis Major or Sirius, etc. Or there are the following interpretations offered by Merkelbach (1984 p. 85):

Degree	Planetary God	Element	Representation in the Tauroctony
1 Corax	Mercury	Air	Raven
2 Nymphus	Venus	Earth	Snake
3 Miles	Mars	-------	Scorpion
4 Leo	Jupiter	Fire	Dog
5 Perses	Moon	Water	Cautopates
6 Heliodromus	Sun	Air	Cautes
7 Pater	Saturn	(Fire)	Mithras

David Ulansey (1989) theorizes that the discovery of the phenomenon of the procession of the equinoxes was a fundamental impetus for the origin of the cult of Mithras. It may be that knowledge of the phenomenon was imported to the West from Iran at about this time. The Magian astrologers were careful observers of the visible sky and would have noted this process centuries earlier.

The function of the Mysteries of Mithras is transformation. The transformation of the world through the unfolding of the mysterious system of the creator's mind and transformation of the individual, his *salvation*, by means of initiation. The vital essences of the bull are the key to salvation: this is why the dog, scorpion and snake are all trying to consume it. Animal sacrifice was not practiced by Mithrists. The bull is connected to the Moon as is the sacred liquid called *hōm* by the Persians of the day. The image of the tauroctony may be a symbolic representation of the extraction of essence from the plants necessary to blend the initiatory drink.

Although Mithraism and Zoroastrianism did not share the same theology, mythology or liturgy they did have many things in common. As we know the Zoroastrians from the time of Zarathustra himself formed what is called the *Mazmaga*, or Great Fellowship. This Fellowship is charged with at least two things: 1) to keep the teachings and traditions of Zarthustra as well as the form of the sacred *manthras* intact, and 2) to insinuate Mazdan teaching into the philosophies and religions of neighboring peoples in a secret and covert way in order to progressively improve conditions in the world and alleviate suffering of the beings of the planet.

Mithraism was exported into the West by the *Mazmaga* and it had the following effects, until it was violently destroyed by Christian thugs and zealots: it provided a place where all men could be equal (whether slave or emperor), it provided a myth and technology for world-transformation, it liberated the soul of the individual to realize his divine-self. In many ways Mithraism functioned much as Freemasonry did in European and American societies of the eighteenth and nineteenth centuries. Wherever we see the action of the Mazmaga it brings balance to the systems it influences: it brings love to the Jews who were bound by Law, it brings equality to the Romans who enslaved and were enslaved, and it will bring to us what we need as well.

Mazdakism
History

Back in Iran itself there was a countercurrent to orthodox Zoroastrian tradition which was to have an impact on the religion in the following years. This was Mazdakism, which has already been discussed from a historical perspective in "A Brief Introduction to the History of Pre-Modern *Eranshahr*" at the beginning of this book.

Because Zoroastrianism is a dynamic and evolving ideology based on an eternal set of principles and fixed verbal foundation (*Avesta*) it can always expect to spawn innovative perspectives. The Mazdakites represent but one of these.

In large measure the Mazdakite school can be seen as a protest movement. Mazdak was protesting against certain social and economic patterns of the Iranian political and religious establishment that ensured that things of value were monopolized by a ruling elite.

During the reign of Dioclitian there appeared in Rome a Manichean by the name of Bundos who taught some rather unique doctrines of the Δαρισθενων (Pah. *dristdênân*, "the adherents of the right religion") while he was there. He also had a student back in Iran named Mazdak. Few details are known about Mazdak except that he was of Iranian background and came from the western parts of the empire.

At the time when Mazdak began his teaching, the Sasanian Empire was in deep turmoil brought on by costly losses in the east in conflicts with the Hephthalites ("White Huns"). These were a nomadic East Iranian people. This caused economic problems which made conditions worse in the empire. Mazdak's vision must be seen in this context. The disparity between the rich and powerful and the poor and powerless was intensified. Also, the Iranians had always practiced polygamy. This meant that the rich, powerful and royal had harems, sometimes quite large. Thus the available women in the country were possessed by a relatively few men. Wealth and property too were increasingly held by a small minority of men. The Persians had even instituted next-of-kin marriage (Pah. *xwēdōdah*), usually with cousins, but also with sisters and even mothers. This was thought to be a highly pious act in Zoroastrianism due to its mythic analogs. However, the economic effect of this was that wealth and property was actually kept in the family. This further solidified the ruling families' control of economic power.

Obviously it was more over these economic threats to the status quo that Mazdak ran afoul of the empire than over his innovative religious doctrines. But for Mazdak these were closely connected. The good thoughts had to find expression in real good actions as well. Mazdak can be called the first true *revolutionary*.

Philosophy

Mazdak is a religious reformer, but true to the unified Mazdan vision in which the spiritual world (*menog*) and the material one (*getig*) are ideally mirrors of one another, and where the "material" universe is no less holy than the "spiritual," Mazdak brought his religious vision into the world of the social and economic order. Most who write about Mazdak do so from the perspective of his social and economic views. While we do not want to ignore these for the reasons given, we do also want to emphasize his religious and even mystical teachings which lie at the root of his ideology.

It was Mazdak's basic assumption that Lord Wisdom had created a world in which all were equal all having what they needed to live natural and happy lives. The inequality that was manifest in the world must be the result of the activity of the *daevas*, evil forces. He identified five principles among these: Envy, Wrath, Vengeance, Need and Greed. Originally the fruits of the earth were shared equally among men, but the mechanisms of the negative principles led the strong to oppress the weak and inequality originated. Mazdak advocated an abolishment of polygamy, next-of-kin marriage and a redistribution of wealth and property evenly throughout the empire.

Mazdak had his own innovative ideas when it came to the theological order. He advocated a simplification of the rituals of Zoroastrianism and emphasized spiritual exercises and ethical action within his cosmological frame of reference. The Neo-Manichean roots of Mazdak's system are shown in the fact that he taught vegetarianism.

For the most part the cosmological order of Mazdak was that of the orthodox Zoroastrians. There is a realm of Light and one of Darkness. The Light is characterized by knowledge, feeling, planned actions and free will whereas Darkness is distinguished by ignorance, insensitivity, random acts of cruelty and coercion.

Mazdak's system was naturally focused on the realm of Light. There are three elements, Fire, Earth and Water. The court of the God of Light is seen as analogous to the court of the Shahânshah where God sits enthroned surrounded by four principle powers, Mind, Intelligence, Memory and Joy. These powers guide the affairs of the world through seven viziers ringed around them, and these are in turn surrounded by a circle of twelve spiritual entities. Obviously these are based on the planetary spheres and the signs of the zodiac. God (Mazda) influences the world though the use of twenty-three letters which are used as keys and levers to universal energies. The aim of the adherent of the Mazdakite faith is the unification of the twenty-three powers, planetary energies, and zodiacal signs. Once this system was realized in the individual, he was made free of religious obligations.

Mansour Shaki, in his insightful article "Cosmogonical and Cosmological Teachings of Mazdak," notes his frustration at not being able to identify an alphabetic system that matches the twenty-three letter system referred to in the records about Mazdakite doctrines. I discovered the table below outlining a version of the Pahlavi alphabet called the "Manichean alphabet" in Hans Jensen's famous book *Sign, Symbol, Script*. It is called Manichean alphabet by many modern scholars because many Manichean texts were written in it. Here we see a version of it where it is made up of *twenty-three* characters. This would also fit with the influence Manicheanism is supposed to have had on Mazdakism.

Manichaean	phonetic value	Manichaean	phonetic value
א	' a	⋈	m
ყ	b	ℓ	n
⅃	g	ഇ	s
﹥ ꝑ	d	⋗	'
א	h	ㅿ	p
ሤ	w	ㅿ̇	f
ᒋ	z	ܖ̈ ܖ̇	q
Ʒ	ž	ܐ ܐ́	r
ზ	ṭ	ω	š
•	j	ᒄ	t
ᗡ ⅃	k	♂	č
Ω	l		

Manichean Alphabet
(Jensen 1969, p. 408)

The Pahlavi alphabet used to write the Middle Persian of Mazdak's day had only twelve basic letters, but at the same time the religious scholars also invented the Avestan script, also called the *Dîn Dabereh*, "religious writing." This latter system had as many as fifty-four letters at its disposal and is one of the most perfect phonetic alphabets ever invented.

Modern scholars are all generally in agreement that although Mazdak was influenced by Manichean doctrines, he did not accept nor teach the idea that the created world, the material universe or human body are evil as Mani did. Mazdak taught an optimistic outlook in keeping with the tenets of the Mazdan Way.

If Mazdak is to be seen as a *saoshyant* of the Mazdan Way it is in that he saw injustice and imbalance in society and in economics and tried to rectify this. He is the first real revolutionary, and like most revolutionaries, their visions are often betrayed by imperfect humans. The course of history and the course of cultural development is corrected over time to accord with their visions, but they, more often than not, end their lives as martyrs.

Mazdakite Echoes
The *Khorramis*

Mazdakism not only had a long-term reforming effect on orthodox Zoroastrianism, it also had various echoes in subsequent sects originating in the old territories of the Sasanian Empire of Persia after the Arabic conquest. These would include the Ishmailis (Assassins) and the less well known Khorramis— who practiced "joyous religion."

This history of Iran shows that there were several movements from within what often at first glance appeared to be Islam but which were really barely disguised Zoroastrian insurgencies. These tended to originate in remote and rural areas of the land. One of these arose in western Iran at the beginning of the Abbisid caliphate led by a man named Sunpadh (the Magus) who came from a village near Nishapur. He was murdered in 755 CE, but the ideology he formulated or merely promulgated continued. The people Sunpadh organized called themselves the *khurramdînân*, "those of the joyous religion." This was a code for Zoroastrianism and/or Mazdakite religion. This term set them apart from the dower, cruel and dark religion of the Arabs. A half century later a new leader arose in the Azerbaijan region named Bâbak (Khorramdîn). He eventually commanded as many as a hundred thousand men and held the entire army of the Abbisid caliphate at bay for over twenty years from his mountain strongholds. In the end Bâbak was betrayed and cruelly executed.

What did the Khorramites believe?

In general it is known that the Khorramite theology was essentially Zoroastrian with a realm of light opposed to one of darkness. This world is good and characterized by Light. This Light was present in all sentient beings and was circulated by natural processes. Everything that was endowed with this Light was capable of feeling pain. Darkness is ignorant and blind, the Light is wise and full of life.

They had inevitably absorbed a good deal of Islamic lore and had become involved in the apparently endless melodramas surrounding the rise and fall of various leaders who argued about their lineages. But this seems to have been more window-dressing rather than substance of belief or practice.

The Khorramis cannot be said to be an organized cult or sect *per se*. Thus they had no unified teaching or doctrine that could be said to hold absolutely true for all Khorramis throughout the land, but they all do seem to hold certain common ideas. These stemmed from indigenous rural Iranian beliefs and practices, and can be seen as analogous to rural "heathens" in early Christian Europe. They appear in one form or another everywhere throughout the region of the old empire, but especially in the mountainous regions.

Those who professed the Joyous Religion saw no clear distinctions between the human and animal, or human and natural worlds insofar as they are animated by the Light. This Light interpenetrates everything and makes everything *alive*. The structure of their cosmology is largely orthodox Zoroastrianism, although they have absorbed certain aspects of Manichean lore without falling into the negativity inherent in orthodox Manicheanism.

The Khorramis also believed in divine incarnation. That is that a person could receive a divine or angelic spirit and then pass it on after he dies to another man. In this way great leaders who were killed could be immortal within the sect or group. At the root of these beliefs is the ancient Iranian idea of the *khwarrenah*, or "glory." It became mixed with Judaic, Christian and Islamic ideas over time. This belief is known as *tanâsok* in Persian or *holul* in Arabic.

To a certain extent the belief in reincarnation, or metempsychosis, represents a logical outgrowth of the idea that the spirit of the individual *needs* to have a body in order to exist as a separate entity. It can enter newly born individuals, in some cases enter adults in the process of *tanâsok* mentioned above, or even enter into animals. The heavenly rewards or hellish punishments for good or bad deeds in life are made manifest in these incarnations— good ones for good actions, bad ones quite naturally for bad ones. The belief in reincarnation is also a strong element in the Druze religion.

The Khorramis practiced non-violence, except when the official banner of revolt (a red flag) was raised in which case violence can be unleashed on one's enemy. Killing a person opposed to the truth and the good is a kindness because the killing liberates them from their bodies which has so polluted their spirits that they have become hopeless. In general they practiced kindness toward all living beings, especially animals. They were vegetarians. The vegetarianism stemmed partly from the impetus toward non-violence and partially due to the fact that they believed the dead flesh of the animal was obviously imbued with *darkness*, so its consumption would represent a spiritually destructive act for the consumer.

Outsiders, especially those of the orthodox Muslim faith, emphasized the antinomian aspects of Khorrami practice. It is said that they do not follow Islamic law, do not observe the dietary practices, have no mosques in their villages (except for visitors). It is unclear as to whether they are merely following their age-old ways regardless of Islam, or whether they are actively rebelling against Islamic norms. Both were probably true to one degree of another. The concept of an individual reaching a perfected angelic or god-like state to become a "man of Paradise," while he still lived, was known to them. They were highly concerned with standards of purity and cleanliness. Their ideas concerning marriage and women was also tinged with antinomianism. It was said that "women are like wells, anyone can drink from them." Wives were shared between brothers and within the village, but only with the consent of the women involved.

In the final analysis both the earlier Mazdakite movement and the later post-Islamic Khorramis appear to have stemmed from rural Iranian belief and practice and been connected to the age-old ways of the common Iranian folk. These ideas had deep roots and they still live. As a matter of fact the Khorramite way and its leaders continue to be held up as heroic ideals into the modern age in various places in Central Asia.

The ideas inherent in Zoroastrianism not only directly made an impact on the world's major religions — Judaism, Christianity, Islam, Buddhism — they also gave rise to many sects and smaller religions within the Islamic world, e.g. the Yezidis, Druzes, Ishmailis, all of which are sill living systems, and many more that have faded away. To this can also be added a number of Sufi schools influenced by Zoroastrian concepts, especially the Illuminist school of Suhrawardi. Adherents of the Occidental Temple of the Wise Lord research these echoes and influences of the Mazdan Way in the history of ideas to enrich our spiritual lives and religious institutions.

Conclusion on Misconceptions

Some of the greatest sources of misconception surrounding the Mazdan Way are the great age of the tradition (much can happen in four thousand years), the tremendous level of tolerance the Mazdans have had for different points of view which allows for variation within the tradition, and the fact that what was the world's most well-known and imitated religion has become a small minority demographically.

Many misconceptions also stem from the identity between the Mazdan Way and Persia. Given the dramatic events of Persian or Iranian history of the last several decades many contemporary people have a difficult time separating the glories of the ancient Persian civilization from the excesses of the Islamic Republic of Iran.

It must also be said that some of the greatest misconceptions surrounding Persian culture are those fostered by the mass media and the world of entertainment. Films such as *300* and its sequel(s) portray ancient Persian culture and religion in ways that are highly inaccurate and misleading, more as an effort to entertain than propagandize, I am sure. However, the present Iranian government, ever sensitive to such things, once lodged a formal complaint about the portrayal of the Persians in this series of films.

One minor, and perhaps unconscious, misconception that has begun to creep into the picture over recent years in the West is that somehow Zoroastrianism, or Mazdaism, is connected with, related to. or in one way or another a part of, *Islam.* Of course, for those familiar with history this is a shocking idea. Mazdans were early *victims* of Islamic conquest and repression. The misconception arises because Mazdaism originates in the Iranian cultural realm and Iran was the single most important empire to be conquered by the Muslims. To the outsider's mind the conquered and the conqueror have often become confused. Clearly the Mazdan Way predates Islam by many, many centuries. But Islam did assimilate many Mazdan beliefs and practices both before the Arabic conquest of Iran and even more afterward. This assimilation process did not occur by accident. The early Arabic/Islamic conquerers were not very learned people in the usual or classical sense. Literacy was new to them. They were almost completely devoid of philosophical acumen. All of this they quickly acquired directly from the long-civilized Persians, who in many ways *re-created* Islam within their own frame of reference. The two major criteria for remaining "Islamic" was 1) the new culture had to be expressed primarily though the *Arabic* language, and 2) the *Qur'an* had to be the primary basis of spiritual culture. Initially these two criteria made the expression of Iranian ideology quite difficult. It was a great creative act on the part of Iranians to infuse Islamic tradition with Persian ideals. The result was mixed. After several generations, by about the year 1000 the Persian language had regained a philosophical voice, and Firdowsi's *Shahnameh* restored some of Persia's own tradition in epic form and did so in the Persian language. The cultural and philosophical struggle between Arabic/Semitic *Islam* (= "Submission") and Iranian (Indo-European) *Dên* ("Insight") is a real and ongoing one.

IV. Jesus— the Zoroastrian

Was Jesus of Nazareth a Zoroastrian or Magian missionary among the Jews? It is impossible to answer this question objectively or with any recourse to historical facts, as few if any historical facts exist relating to the person of Jesus. We only have documents written by those charged with creating a religion around his personality and others by those attacking these efforts, both among the Jews and pagan Romans. Additionally all of these documents were for the most part written at the earliest decades after the events occurred, that is, if they occurred at all.

Several writers and commentators have made the bold assertion that Jesus was a Zoroastrian. One of these, Derreck Evanson, has written a treatise on the subject called "Jesus was a Zoroastrian!" (zoroastrian.angelfire.com) and founded a neo-Zoroastrian movement called The Friends of God International. Additionally, elsewhere on the Internet, many articles and sites can be found which argue for and against the idea that Zoroastrianism is the starting point of Christianity and/or Judaism itself. These can be read and studied by those more deeply interested in this topic. The OTWL recognizes Jesus as a Saoshyant, but considers his mission to have been betrayed by many of the organization(s) founded after his death. Our purpose and mission is driven solely from within the innate goodness of the Mazdan principles, without regard to "historical" arguments. We do not tend to *argue* history or dogma. This is perhaps because we know that our way is rooted in the oldest authentic spiritual path and that others have tried to imitate it, but have always fallen short of the standards of Mazdan insight, reason and spiritual power. Besides, we do not believe in arguing spiritual matters, as this practice quickly slides off into attempts to coerce the other side into believing what we believe. Others will come to the Truth, not based on coercion and argument, but only through education and experience. This code proved to be a disadvantage to Mazdans in the great battle of creeds over the centuries. Those creeds which have put the conquest (winning) of souls above the Truth have generally succeeded in the geopolitical realm. But we cannot alter our principles. To do so would be the final triumph of the *daevas*. This is something which logically cannot occur.

In the next three sections we will explore different topics relating to the question of the possible Mazdan context of the figure of Jesus of Nazareth. In all that is said here it must always be remembered that there are two different Jesuses present at all times: one, the possible historical man and what he may or may not have taught and done, and two, the mythic figure reported in various forms of "scripture" and theological treatises.

Mazdan Reinvention of Judaism

Some have logically objected that the whole myth and meaning of Jesus and Christianity are first and foremost only explicable from within the constructs of Judaism and that any explanation of Christianity or the message of Jesus from a Mazdan angle is absurd. They have a good point in the sense that the historical Jesus, if he existed at all, would have explained things and taught entirely from within what appears to be the Judaic myth or frame of reference. This logical argument neglects the possibility that Judaism itself is a bungled attempt to imitate Persian ideas. Many of the most important doctrines of Judaism are of Iranian origin: monotheism, the idea of a messiah, an end of time and establishment of an earthy paradise, and even the resurrection of the dead.

We think of the Jews as monotheists, and many ignorantly believe that the Jews invented the concept of monotheism. This is categorically untrue. This can be proven from within biblical texts when we see that the first of the so-called "Ten Commandments" is "Thou shalt have no *other* gods *before* me." Clearly other gods were recognized as existing, it was just that Jehovah wanted to be "number one." Zarathustra makes it clear that there *is no other god* but the Wise Lord, and that all other entities "worthy of worship" (*yazatas*) are derived from this one principle. The Jews of the pre-Babylonian period were not given to scholarly pursuits nor to mystical speculation. This they absorbed during the Babylonian period and under the guidance of the Persians. The religion was totally reformed during and after this period. The very concept of philosophical monotheism is of Iranian origin and was only gradually and imperfectly absorbed by the Hebrews over time.

In 586 BCE Israel was conquered by the Babylonians and the population of Israel was relocated in the Mesopotamian region. This is referred to as the "Babylonian Captivity." The Jews were free and many of them rose to high ranks in the Babylonian state. At this time in Babylon Persian ideas were being absorbed from their neighbors to the east. Among these ideas were the religious doctrines of the Zoroastrians. The Jews were apparently very open to being influenced by these ideas, as were most peoples when they were exposed to them. In 358 Babylon was conquered by Cyrus the Great and became part of the Persian Empire. A year later the Jews were given permission to return to Israel to rebuild their temple which had been destroyed by the Babylonians. Cyrus is seen as a *messiah* in Jewish tradition, and is the only man so named in their literature. Of course, this is probably because the very idea of a *messiah* as a savior was adopted from the Persians! Many Jews remained behind in the Persian Empire and did not return to Jerusalem. It was during these years, and in this cultural melieu that Judaism was totally reformed. The Hebrew alphabet was adopted, the Talmudic literature was written, the traditions of the prophets established, the Torah was revised and rewritten into the canonical form it has today. The myth of the Garden of Eden was adopted at this time and the Book of Genesis written. Doctrines about monotheism, the *messiah* as savior, angelology and demonology, resurrection of the dead, a final paradise on earth... These are but a few of the reforms and additions that took place under Persian influence. This influence was probably the result of friendly personal relationships between Jewish scribes and sages and Zoroastrian priests.

This marked the beginning of a wonderful friendship between the Jewish and Persian peoples. Cyrus is seen as a liberator and teacher of the Jews. Typical of the way Cyrus worked, he allowed others to think he was being influenced by them, rather than the other way around. The fact that the Jews adopted so many Persian ideas, yet the Persians do not seem to have been similarly influenced is testimony to the truth of the matter. Even in Christian doctrine Cyrus (Koresh) is seen as what is called a "prefiguration" of Christ.

The *Magoi* and the Young Jesus

Assuming that Jesus was a historical figure, which some have been led to doubt, he would have been born sometime around the beginning of the Common Era. The place of his birth was in Judea, traditionally in Bethlehem. The Gospel accounts make it clear that Jesus was not visited by the *magoi*, or Wise Men, at the time of his nativity, but some months or even years after that. The best guess is that he would have been about two years old. This also fits with Herod's order to kill all boy children under two years of age in order to kill whatever boy who was prophesied to usurp him.

These *magoi* are generally held to be Zoroastrian priests who were also astrologers. From their observations of the sky they predicted that a savior, in their terms a *saošyant*, was to be born in the kingdom of Israel at around the time of Jesus' birth. The nature of the observation they made cannot be known for sure. It was most probably a conjunction of some kind, or a nebula or comet that appeared in a constellation that signified the country of Israel. In this way they would have known the approximate time and location of the birth in question. It is known that Persian astrologers were the first to cast natal horoscopes of the kind we are used to today. These sages set out from their sanctuary and star-observatory to make contact with this child and give him gifts. Some discussions of these events try to make it seem like this was a great expedition and an arduous journey. In fact for people from their culture this would have been a short and easy trip. The Iranians had been conducting caravans from Egypt to India and from China to Mesopotamia for centuries. The *magoi* likely traveled from either Mesopotamia or the mountainous regions of the Caucuses to Israel.

In the region of Israel the political world of the day was one divided between two great empires: the Romans in the west and the Parthians in the east. The Parthians had re-Iranianized the empire that Alexander the Great had created three centuries before. The Parthians had held the religion of Israel as a part of their empire just a few decades before the time of Jesus and the puppet king of Israel, Herod, was on friendly terms with the Parthians as well as the Romans. This explains why the Zoroastrian priests were received by the king in the Gospel story, as we shall see.

The three Wise Men became a favorite icon of Christian tradition over the centuries. The tradition in the West gave them the names Caspar, Melchior and Balthazar. An Eastern tradition, probably closer to any facts that might have existed, knows them by their Persian names: Hormizdh, Yazdegerd and Perozadh. Tradition has it that they were of different ages, Hormizdh being a young man, Yazdegerd in his middle years, and Perozadh being an elderly man. All three names are Persian. In medieval Germany there was a virtual cult of the Magi. Its exact nature is unknown, however, a monument to it comes in the form of one of the greatest edifices of medieval Germany: the Cathedral of Cologne. It was built to house the supposed relics of the three Wise Men. Over the church, instead of the usual cross, there is a golden Star.

But let us return to the time of the birth of Jesus. By the time of Jesus the Persianization process of the post-Captivity period in Judaism had developed a long history. Jews were divided into three camps by then: the Sadducees, Pharisees and Essenes. The Sadducees believed in the literal meaning of the Torah (Bible), that there was no after-life, that the ritual of the temple was the essence of the religion. The Pharisees believed in an oral tradition beside the Torah, that the Torah was subject to learned interpretation (Talmud), that there would be a resurrection with eternal life, the good would be rewarded the wicked punished and they also believed in individual prayer and assembly in houses of worship (synagogues). The Essenes were a mystical ascetic sect who were disgusted with both of the other two and lived monastic lives in the desert. The Pharisees are identified as the "Persian faction" who accepted the reforms that came about in Babylon due to Persian influence. The word Pharisee is probably derived form "Persian." The Essenes were a tiny minority, the Sadducees were the vast majority (over ninety percent of the population adhered to this faction) and the Pharisees were a sizable minority. In any event, only the Pharisees were equipped to survive the destruction of the Second Temple in 70 CE by the Romans. All of modern Judaism is derived from this Persian branch of the Pharisees.

Jesus may have been critical of the Pharisees on many occasions, but it was to their camp that he belonged. His influence and preaching was oriented toward fulfilling the essence of the reforms first begun in Babylon in the Talmudic Age.

Another tradition holds that the Essenes were derived from an older sect called the Magusseans who bore the lineage of Daniel who had been named the Rab-Mag by the Persian emperor.

In any event at the time the Gospels were being written the international prestige of the Iranian religious traditions was as strong as ever. The Magians were known as the masters of all sorts of religious knowledge. The story of the three magi, Zarathustrian priests, who used some sort of stellar science to determine that a savior, or the savior, had been born in the area of Israel at a certain point in time, whether true or not would have been used by the Gospel writers to add prestige to the story of Jesus. It was important for the new religion of Christianity to get the seal of approval from the most prestigious authorities on religion in the world— the *magi*, the priests of Mazda. This is the real message and importance of the story of the journey of the three *magi* and their visit to the young Jesus.

The idea that these men were "kings" is a later medieval development of Christian propaganda. They were made to be kings of the three major regions of the world: Europe, Asia and Africa. The African heritage of the third king is responsible for his representation as having darker skin than the other two. Again this is mere Church propaganda to make it seem that the world world recognized the godhood of Jesus and that he was the King of Kings (i.e. the Iranian formula for "emperor" [*šahânšah*]). Clearly the Gospel story actually represents them as priests (*magoi*) with astrological knowledge, not as "kings." All the Gospel of Matthew intends to convey is that the Iranian priests, the greatest arbiters of religion of the day, held the person of Jesus in esteem and thought of him as a savior, or *saošyant*.

As very few facts are known of the life of Jesus outside the literature created by his latter-day followers, almost anything is historically possible. Subsequent history seems to show that his original mission and teaching was betrayed by later followers who either did not learn from him directly (e.g. Paul or Jesus' brother James) or did not understand his teaching completely, or willfully altered the significance of it to create a program for mischief. Perhaps the best way to come to any understanding of this is to look at the significance of the teachings in a greater context.

It is our preferred interpretation that Jesus was a missionary of the Mazdan way to the Jews and that the group to which he belonged the Nazarenes were a sect descended from the Magusseans with continuing direct links to Persia. We would not suggest that Jesus was trying to teach orthodox Zoroastrianism, or that he was trying to articulate his ideas from within any context other than the local understandings of religion at the time. But in essence and meaning he was bringing a new insight to the system and the effect of his life and death had a profound impact on the local population.

The often heard title of Jesus being "Jesus of Nazareth" is misleading because although there is a town named Nazareth on the map in Israel *now*, there was no such town in the time of Jesus. The area where the town was later erected was indeed called Nazareth, but it was at the time an uninhabited ancient grave yard. The Greek proper adjective used to apply to the name of Jesus was Ναζαραιος, "Nazarene," never is the word used to name a town. It is a sect and not a town that is being referenced.

I will leave it to some more interested and qualified party to make a systematic study of the possibilities of this theory and of the following characteristics that indicate the plausibility of this theory. The whole history of Christianity is one based on the misunderstood, misapplied and misused interpretation of the life and teachings of the founder. This stems from two things: the founder (Jesus) may not have been trying to found a new religion and the religion that was founded in his name was one motivated by the acquisition of power and control above all other considerations.

The Meaning and Mission of Jesus

Given the historical circumstances it is difficult to determine what the mission of Jesus was exactly. The best assumption is that it was an effort to reform the Judaic religion by bringing new elements into it, and by fulfilling trends that had been instituted into Judaism from the time of the Babylonian Captivity, from the time of the Talmud. The organizations (churches) established after his death developed in directions his teachings do not seem to indicate.

In this section we will consider things which seem to be ideas taught by Jesus, mythic paradigms enacted by his actions, and developments from his teachings that do not seem to be entirely motivated by coercive utility wielded by organized Christianity.

<u>The End of Animal Sacrifice:</u> One interesting aspect of the mission of Jesus which is perhaps the most essential from the standpoint of Christian ideology, but which often goes unnoticed from the Zoroastrian perspective is the abolition of animal sacrifice which the mythic interpretation of the death of Jesus instituted. Zarathustra opposed animal sacrifice on two counts: 1) the cruelty to the soul of the ox (the animal soul) and 2) the sacrifices being practiced by the warrior class in his own day were seen as being excessive and therefore evil.

Before going any further, however, we need to review what is meant by "animal sacrifice" in the two traditions in question: the Indo-European and the Hebraic.

The Indo-European sacrifice, of the kind the cult out of which Zoroastrianism emerged around thirty-seven hundred years ago, would sacrifice an animal in a quick and relatively painless way, divide the animal parts into two categories: 1) the parts that humans wanted to eat and 2) the parts they did not want to eat. The latter were deemed to be the portion to be given to the gods. Typically these were the heads, forelegs, internal organs, etc. These parts were deposited in the earth, water, or burned. The different gods and goddesses demanded different rituals. The meat from the animal was then consumed by humans in a convivial meal in which the gods shared. In a manner of speaking these rituals were sacralized versions of the normal process of butchering animals for consumption. Zarathustra's complaint was that it was excessive, and this probably meant that more animals were being killed than could be eaten. The over all purpose of the Indo-European animal sacrifice is the exchange of gifts between men and gods, to commune with the gods and to bind the tribe to its gods ritually.

By contrast the purpose of the Hebraic animal sacrifice was the *forgiveness of sins*. Before the destruction of the Second Temple in Jerusalem in 70 CE, the Judaic cult was centered on this temple complex and its activities. One of the main activities of this complex was animal sacrifice. The procedure went like this: a man would bring an animal (a goat, but most usually a *lamb*) and mount the sacrificial altar in the courtyard of the temple. There he would be met with a sacrificial priest who had him confess his sins while laying his hand on the animal. His sin was thought to be transferred to the blood of the animal. The priest would then cut the throat of the animal and allow the blood to run off of the altar in gutters around its edges. The blood was then thought to be "unclean." The body of the animal was then transferred to the brazen altar (a furnace) where the body would be consumed as a burnt offering to Jehovah.

This context shows a number of things: The types of animal sacrifice practiced by the Indo-Europeans and the Hebrews had little in common. The death of Jesus was mythologized to make the sacrifice of his life a substitute for all future animal sacrifices in the Judaic context. He became the Lamb of God, i.e. a substitute for the sacrificial lambs through the sacrifice of which the contemporary Jews had their sins washed away or forgiven. So the meaning of Jesus' death was the end of the necessity of animal sacrifice. With the destruction of the temple in Jerusalem this type of cultic activity ceased as well and the Jews began to worship with prayer in synagogues in the manner of the Pharisees teachings.

Other major features of Christianity which could very well stem from the Mazdan Way are:

<u>Balance</u>: I would not be the first to observe that Jesus seems to be on a mission to bring balance to the world of the contemporary Jews. He

found a world bound by considerations of Law (*Torah*) lacking in Love. Some have speculated that his Word, his operating formula, was Αγαπη ("Love"). In attempting this he is applying the Mean, the principle of balance between extremes which is one of the most important Mazdan principles, and one which we have seen several times in these essays.

Individual Salvation: One of the main tenets of Zoroastrianism is that the individual is a sovereign entity and is destined for perfection and immortality as an individual. This is one of the most revolutionary ideas that Jesus attempted to introduce to the Judaic world. The Jews, then as now, believe in a collective "salvation" or a coming age of resurrected righteous people, but this will only come to the whole of the Jewish population as a group, not as individuals. The very idea of a final resurrection was not unanimously agreed upon in the time of Jesus by all Jews. Some believed in no after-life at all as we have seen. The ideas of a coming messiah and the final resurrection of the dead are both ideas imported into Judaism from Iran. But Jesus teaches the revolutionary idea of individual salvation.

Emphasis of Good versus Evil: One of the practices for which Jesus is best known is his magical ability to cast out evil, or "unclean," spirits. This is a common formula in the New Testament, but is only alluded to once in the Old Testament, and is not connected to the magical practice. Clearly this was not a common Jewish belief or practice, but one which Jesus emphasized in his mission. This is obviously an influence from the Zoroastrian ideology of *yazatas* and *daevas* (or angels and demons) being influential in people's lives. It is actually a sophisticated understanding of the *daevas* to model them as dysfunctional paradigms or mechanisms, such as a disability of the mind, eye or limb, rather than as an imp or personalized, anthropomorphized, spirit. By the same token in Christian belief the idea of an angel was one of a spiritual entity, like it is in Zoroastrianism, rather than the almost materialistic entity that seem to be often described in the Old Testament where they appear as "men." See for example Genesis 18.2 and 19.16.

The now familiar concept of God and his angels locked in mortal combat with the forces of Satan which culminates in Christian mythology in the visionary text called Revelation is only possible with the influence of Iranian models. The old Jewish concept of Satan is reflected in the Book of Job. There we seen God and Satan on friendly terms, taking bets on whether Satan can make Job lose his faith in God... In the old Jewish concept Satan is the one who prosecutes man in the court of God, but he is still an "officer of the court." In the religion of Jesus Satan has been recast into a pure opponent of all that is good, into the image of Angra Mainyu.

Zoroastrianism has a clear idea of heaven and hell. Other religions adopted this idea, and Christianity perhaps emphasized it more than the other religions. Jesus himself does not seem to dwell on this idea, but the organized church which was to follow did. They did so in a misguided way, but an effective way for their purposes: power and control. The original Mazdan function of hell is a place of punishment for misdeeds (bad thoughts, bad word, bad actions) but it it not eternal. It lasts as long as is necessary. The Zoroastrians envision that there would even be guardians to oversee the punishments so that none is more severe than the misdeed warrants. For the Zoroastrian hell is a place of painful purification and a place for the leveling of debts. Some sects, which believed in reincarnation, just placed the soul of the hell-bound individual in an undesirable body and life. The merit a living person gains by being kind to others is connected to this idea. In Christian dogma hell becomes a place of eternal punishment and damnation. This is a doctrine that was promulgated as a control mechanism. The Church attempted to control human behavior through fear, just as most religions have used this idea. The temptation to use it this way was just too great to forego given their lust for power and control. The Zoroastrian doctrine just seems based on a certain metaphysical logic: Ahura Mazda created Man whom he provided with the power of choice between good and evil, man volunteers to incarnate on earth to fight for good against evil, sometime man misuses the freedom of choice and does bad. For each of these bad actions there is a reflex action, now or later. Debts are incurred and must be paid. If the individual is judged at the Chinvat Bridge to have done more good than bad, he or she will pass on and the punishing river of fire will feel like a bath in warm milk. These are all poetic metaphors to express the idea that the true practitioner of *humata-huxta-hwarshta* will be alleviated from the punishments, not by the unearned "grace" of God, but due to the good choices made in life.

Jesus certainly emphasized the love and care for the weakest members of society, the "poor," if you will. This attitude was first expressed by Zarathustra in his desire to protect the poor, the defenseless, the helpless creatures, the environment, etc. This attitude, in the case of the Zarahtustran is born of strength. The truly strong do not despise the weak. To despise something is to fear it on some level. The Mazdan strives to be fearless, and thus without hate.

The Lord's Prayer and the Mazdan Way

Contrary to what we see practiced in Christian churches today, Jesus admonished his followers to pray only in private and then to pray only the prayer that came to be known as "The Lord's Prayer," or the "Our Father." This is found in the new Testament Book of Matthew (6.9-13) An analysis of that text reveals the system of Jesus:

Πατερ.‛ημων ‛ο εν τοις ουρανοις ‛αγιασθητωτο.ονομα.σου ελθετω ‛η βασιλεια.σου γενηθητω το.θελημα.σου, ‛ως εν ουρανω, και επι της γης. τον.αρτον.ημων τον επιουσιον δος ‛ημιν ση–μερον. καιαφεςημιν τα.οφειληματα.‛ημων, ως και ‛ημεις αφιεμεν τοις.οφειλεταις.‛ημων. καιμη.εισενεγκης ‛ημας εις πειρασμον αλλα ρυσαι ‛ημας απο τουπονηρ. οτι σουεστιν ‛η βασιλεια και ‛η δυναμις και ‛η δοξα εις τους αιωνας.

1. Our father
2. who art in heaven
3. sanctified be thy name
4. (let) thy kingdom come
5. (let) thy will be done, in heaven as it is on earth
6. our necessary bread give us today
7, forgive us our debts as we too forgive our debtors
8. lead us not into temptation but deliver us from evil
9. thine is the kingdom, power and glory unto the ages.

1. God. Our Father: Before the mission of Jesus the Jews never thought of God as a "father figure," although this God certainly behaved in their mythology as a dysfunctional father, as in the Myth of the Garden of Eden. However, what Jesus spoke of was the familial and amicable attitude toward God. This is in keeping with the Zoroastrian attitude toward Ahura Mazda: a deity characterized by consciousness as the principle which all humans share and which makes all humans part of one family of sentient and self-aware beings. Jesus regularly speaks directly to his God as a family member and as a friend in a manner very much like the way Zarathustra taught us to do in the Gathas, composed almost two-thousand years before Jesus lived. That Jesus considered everyone to be the sons and daughters of God is shown by the fact that he taught others to pray the "Our Father" prayer. This formula, or at least the *Pater Noster* segment of it was probably part of Mithraic or Magussean practices before it was used by Jesus.

2. Divine Existence beyond the Stars: The deity exists in a realm beyond our immediate cosmos, in the realm of *menog*, beyond the stars.

3 Holy Name: The "name" of God, the verbal formula of the divinity, is a sanctified or holy code. See also the Mazdan Amesha Spenta known as Spenta Mainyu, "holy spirit," and the reference to the Manthra Spenta, "Holy Word" a *yazata* to which the twenty-ninth day of the month is dedicated.

4. Coming Kingdom: This is a reference to the coming state of cosmic salvation, the Frashokereti, or "Making Wonderful" to be ushered in by the last Saoshyant, or "savior."

5. <u>The Unity of Heaven and Earth:</u> The will (Gk. *thelēma*) of the Father is potent and present both in the heavenly and the terrestrial realm. *Menog* and *getik* are reflective of one another in the ideal state. This points to the goodness of the world and the unity of heaven and earth.

6. <u>Provision for our needs by God:</u> Jesus worked as a practicing magician and teacher. He lived day by day, each day receiving what he needed to survive. The divinity provides for us, if we know how to ask.

7. <u>Divine Behavior:</u> The text that follows the prayer clarifies that when man behaves as God does the individual can expect reciprocal behavior from God. We forgive, so God will forgive. This emphasis on the *forgiveness* of things is particularly Judeo-Christian. Nevertheless it speaks to the general theory that man should imitate the ways of God and that the ways of God are kind, forgiving, enlightening, and protective. (Here reference is to the God of the New Testament, of course.)

8. <u>Protection from Evil:</u> This particular line is again especially reflective of Judaic attitudes, as it actually refers to the possibility that God might "lead man into temptation"! This Ahura Mazda would never do. But the wish to be protected from evil is a valuable formula.

9. <u>Kingdom-Power-Glory:</u> This triad seems rooted in the spiritual world of the Mazdans: the kingdom (*khshathra*) is the right ordering of the world, the power (*amal*) is the personal energy to effect one's will, and the glory (*khvarena*) is the famous halo or nimbus of divine authority and good fortune that it attached to people of great ethical accomplishment. The very idea of the "ages" (Gk. *aiones*) was, of course, originated in Iranian cosmology with its succession of ages of the world.

In this prayer, or *manthra*, Jesus sums up his philosophy and teaches it as an encapsulated magical verbal formula. This perhaps explains why the "Pater Noster" was used so much in medieval Christian magic. Although the subsequent builders of the Christian movement probably did not understand what the teachings of Jesus were, and if they did they did their best to obscure them, nevertheless certain passages of text slipped by and have survived to clarify the teachings somewhat.

This essay has been offered in the spirit of building a bridge between the dominant religious paradigm in the West and the Mazdan Way. Most of what has been written here is of a speculative nature, due to the questions surrounding the source materials. The contents of this essay should be taken more as a suggestion as to the direction of the future, rather than an analysis of the past in any purely historical sense.

V. Angels and Demons

It is widely acknowledged that it is within Zoroastrian doctrines that the angelology and demonology of all the Abrahamic religions have their origin. Today many are fascinated by both angels and demons, yet these entities, by whatever name one wishes to call them, are best understood within the mythic construct that originated the idea, rather than ones that just borrowed the concepts in garbled forms for their own purposes.

As we shall see, it appears that the belief in an array of good forces opposed to bad ones is a primeval Indo-European belief. This remained in the realm of unsystematic and pre-philosophical mythology until the advent of the prophetic vision of Zarathustra. Zarathustra took what was vaguely felt or perceived on a mythic level and analyzed the philosophical truth behind it.

The Iranian doctrine is simple and straightforward. It might even be considered logical, because it is rooted in a rational system. Ahura Mazda has a set of *hamkârân*, that is, "co-workers" who are the Amesha Spentas (Holy Immortals) and who are direct emanations of the deity. They are seven in number, beyond these are the *yazatas*, "those worthy of worship." All of these together form an array of major forces on the side of Good. They are paradigms or mechanisms by which the Good is made manifest in the cosmos. In later terminology, these are equated with the Western term "Angels." The Amesha Spentas are called Archangels and the *yazatas* simply "angels." Human beings too have "angelic" natures attached to them. These are the *fravashis*. They guide and protect the individual and are also called "Holy Guardian Angels." To these are opposed in a regular fashion a set of daevic entities. Each responds in a negative or contrary way to the positive creations of Ahura Mazda. In reality Ahura Mazda is not opposed by an equal entity. It is only at the next level down that such opposition can occur.

The Greeks had a preexisting system or set of ideas surrounding the divine entities attached to the gods and men. One of these is called a δαιμων (*daimōn*), from which our word "demon" is derived. As we shall see, in the beginning this was not at all a negative being. The pagan Greeks understood the *daimōn* in a rather neutral way, there could be good ones or bad ones, as we will see. The Christians chose this word to "demonize"— literally. The "demon" became something wholly diabolical or evil. Our word "evil" is derived from Greek διαβολος (*diabolos*): "slanderer, backbiter, enemy; N.T. the Devil." As you can see, the original Greek meaning was simply a slanderer, but the Christians developed the word into one reflecting the role of Satan in their theology. All this being the case they had to have a new word to represent a good daimōn, so the word for "messenger" (Gk.

αγγελος) was used. This is a loan translation for Hebrew *mal'āk* meaning "messenger." It occurs in phrases such as *mal'āk 'elōhīm*, "messenger of God." The cognate word in Arabic is *malāk*, pl. *malā'ikah*, "angel." Both Hebrew and Arabic written sources have many references to such "messengers of god." But these messengers do not always necessarily appear to be supernatural beings, but rather men.

In general, and in the Iranian model angels are individual aspects or extensions of the Divinity each with its own form of existence. As we have seen these were called "messengers" of God (αγγελος) by the Christians but "those worthy of worship" (*yazatas*) by the Iranians. Just as the Good has extensions and messengers (i.e. substructures and paradigms) by which it functions in the world and in humanity, so too does the Bad. These bad mechanisms are poetically called *daevas* by the Iranians. The Greek philosophers and magicians sometimes called one type of these entities a αγαθω–δαιμων, "good *daimōn*" and the other a κακο–δαιμων, bad *daimōn*.

If we consult the standard Greek dictionary, that of Liddle and Scott (1982, pp. 365-6), we find the following definitions of the word δαιμων (*daimōn*): "god, goddess; Divine power, power controlling the destiny of individuals; good or evil geniuses of men or women;" in the plural *daimones*, "the souls of men of the golden age acting a tutelary deities; spiritual or divine being inferior to the gods" Also noted is the αγαθος δαιμων, ('good daimōn'), "the Good Genius to which a toast was drunk after dinner." The word *daimōn* can be either masculine or feminine.

There is also another derivative Greek word δαιμονιον (*daimonion*) with about the same meanings, basically the "divine power, or inferior divine being; genius." This word is grammatically neuter.

Here we clearly see that the original Greek meaning of the term *daimōn* was either a purely good one, or at least neutral. It answers fairly closely to the Iranian *fravashi* or the Germanic *fylgja*. Only in Christian terminology is it saddled with a negative connotation. The Christians brought in a Greek word for "messenger" (αγγελος) for the "good daimōn."

Often some people seem put off by the Mazdan identification and characterization of the *daevas* as *evil* entities. Some try to invoke a "non-dualistic" viewpoint and refer to Hindu thought! The fact is that Hindus as well did the same thing, they "demonized" some *asuras* (Av. *ahuras*) and made the *devas* (Av. *daevas*) the good entities. The point is both realize that there is a division of paradigmatic activity in the cosmos, one beneficial and good, the other detrimental and bad. The same thing is found in other Indo-European systems, e.g. in the Germanic world where we find gods (whether *æsir* and *vanir*) and evil

73

entities called *thursar*. There too the world is seen as a battleground between forces of good and evil, between life and death, between the beneficial and conscious opposed to the detrimental and non-conscious. The thing that distinguishes and intensifies the Mazdan system is that it is so aware, systematic and *philosophically* based that it is impossible to squirm out of the consequences intellectually.

The Truth about Angels is this: they are positive and beneficial mechanisms, paradigms or constructs of thought, word or deed which influence sentient beings toward the Good. They are great in number and power. The prevailing operative mechanism of the cosmos is guided by such angels or *yazatas*. The Mazdan *worships* them by performing rituals made up of good thoughts, words and actions which support the continuing and evolving effects of these constructs. Other forms of worship include ethical action and everyday mental discipline and enjoyment of life. These mechanisms are clothed with forms by our imaginations which make them easier to deal with, easier to communicate with, if you will.

The Truth about Daevas is this: they are negative and detrimental mechanisms, paradigms or constructs of thought, word or deed which influence sentient beings toward the Bad. They are few in number and low power. The prevailing operative mechanism of the cosmos is guided by such *daevas*, or *yazatas*. The Mazdan *fights against* them by performing rituals made up of good thoughts, words and actions which block the interfering effects of these constructs. Their effects are also thwarted by ethical action and everyday mental discipline and enjoyment of life. These mechanisms are given forms by our imaginations which make them easier to identify, name and then defeat.

Why Western Demons are often Angels, or how "Satanism" became a Religion in the West

How can there be a religion called "Satanism"? To the Mazdan mind the worship or honoring of Angra Mainyu is something that is akin to certifiable insanity. How can one wish to bring more ignorance, stupidity, violence, poverty and sickness into one's life— which the "worship" of Angra Mainyu would do? The answer is, of course, that the demons of the West are not the *daevas* of the East.

In the dominant religion of the West, Christianity, the creator god is saddled with the Edenic myth, where it appears that Adonay is an oppressor god who punishes and abuses his creation for daring to desire knowledge and immortality based on their own efforts. For this reason the instigator/educator, the Serpent (Lucifer?), can seen in an *heroic* Light. Orthodox "demons" are easily seen as heroic rebels against an oppressive god of unreason and violence. Most Judeo-Christian demons can be seen, and are seen in the practice of magic, as able to provide benefits, certain powers and special knowledge. Additionally, it was the standard Christian strategy to demonize all of the old gods of the nations as they were Christianized. So from within Christian myth the demons can be seen as pro-human heroes, and all of the people's old divinities were demonized leaving people feeling disenfranchised and oppressed. For all of these reasons there grew up in the West an urge toward what can be called "Satanism." As soon as Adonay is unmasked, a new understanding of his adversary is realized. A similar paradigm existed in pre-Christian Greek mythology, where the chief god, Zeus was an oppressor, and his opponent, the titan, Prometheus, a pro-human bringer of the Fire of Consciousness. For those who are interested in this discussion, I recommend my book *Lords of the Left-Hand Path* (Inner Traditions, 2012). In many ways the practice of Satanism is a reversion to the old meaning of the *daimōn*, as a personal genius. Practices and beliefs which strengthen and develop this personal genius are good, but contrary to orthodox Christian doctrine, hence to be condemned as pagan or diabolical by them, and to be involved with the so-called left-hand path.

Let us now pose the question: Is the Mazdan Way a left-hand path tradition?

In order to answer this question I will lay out the same definition I did in my book *Lords of the Left-Hand Path*, originally written in 1993. Then we will examine this in terms of the Zarathustran revolution of over three thousand years ago. In that book I noted two major criteria: self-deification and antinomianism.

> There are two major criteria for being considered a true [practitioner of the left-hand path]— Deification of the Self and Antinomianism. The first of these is complex: The system of thought proposed by the magician or philosopher must be one that promotes individual self-deification, preferably based on an initiatorily magical scheme. This first criterion will be seen to have four distinct elements:
>
> 1) Self-deification— attainment of an enlightened (or awakened), independently existing intellect and its relative immortality.
> 2) Individualism— the enlightened intellect is that of a given individual, not a collective body
> 3) Initiation— the enlightenment and strength of essence necessary for the desired state of evolution of self are attained by means of stages created by the will of the magician, not because he or she was "divine" to begin with.
> 4) Magic— practitioners of the left-hand path see themselves as using their own wills in a rationally intuited system or spiritual technology designed to cause the universe around them to conform to their self-willed patterns.

The second criterion, antinomianism, states that practitioners think of themselves as "going against the grain" of their culturally conditioned and conventional norms of "good" and "evil." A true [practitioner of the left-hand path] will have the spiritual courage to identify himself with the cultural norms of "evil." There will be an embracing of the symbols of conventional "evil," or "impurity," or "rationality," or whatever quality the conventional culture fears and loathes. The lord of the left-hand path will set himself apart from his fellow man, will actually or figuratively become an outsider, in order to gain the kind of inner independence necessary for the other initiatory work present in the first criterion. The practice of this second criterion often manifests itself in "antinomianism," that is, the purposeful reversal of conventional normatives.

When we look at the four major elements of the practice of the first criterion we discover a mixed result: Self-deification is a process of realization and remembrance of one's divine origin and identity. The idea of individualism is highly emphasized in the Mazdan Way, each person possesses a unique *fravashi*. The concept of initiation is strongly present, but it is almost a given that one is first initiated into the basic understanding, then it will be up to the individual to attain to the higher levels of being a *magavan* or *athravan*. The stages are there, but the institution does not emphasize these, the states of being either are, or are not present for all to see and recognize. As regards the practice of magic in this process: it is, of course, present because the very art and practice of Mazdan worship is the spiritual technology of the *magavan* or magician.

Finally, as regards the idea of antinomianism: The time of antinomianism is somewhat past for the Mazdan. In ancient times it was strong: when members of the Mazmaga were struggling against the unphilosophical and crude worship of the daevas by the established authorities. The degree to which one lives in a culture or society which honors and upholds negative paradigms as paragons of virtue is the degree to which one can practice antinomianism. If you work in an industry devoted to deception, you might want to rebel. If you exist in a society filled with ignorance and cruelty, you might want to rebel. But there is no need to revolt against an established order just for the sake of rebelling. Antinomianism is a reaction to injustice in the established order. Your conscience must be your guide.

So in answer to the question concerning the left-hand path nature of the Mazdan Way: In some ways the Mazdan Way *defines* the left-hand path— it is the realization of the divinity of the individual with a promise of a return to the ever-young enjoyments of the flesh through the progressive application of the technology of the *magavan*. But perhaps because of its deep roots, its age old mythology and theology in which the God of the system is seen both as the established deity and one which is entirely deserving of our worship and honor, the rebellion is never against the Wise Lord, but rather only against the societal effects of the enemies of the Wise Lord that the question of antinomianism is ameliorated.

In the final analysis, the whole question of angels and demons and of the right or left-hand path are all extremely secondary. The Mazdan Way is what it always has been as defined in its own terms, not in terms of other things. Such discussions as we have had here are only useful to those who are trying to understand the Mazdan Way from an outside perspective, which is often the perspective one has to take in preparation for entering into the way directly. There are many doorways in the hall, all open to the Truth.

At this point I wish to stress to the critical reader that I am not engaging in a tortured argument to reverse a prevailing and established truth. Rather I am attempting to restore logic and reason to a myth that has already undergone more than its share of such twisting and distortion. God is wise, kind and good, not vengeful, angry and jealous. God wants Man himself to be wise, strong and good and eventually to take his place in the circle of divinity. God joyfully gives Man the tools he needs to complete the struggle and the work. Christian myth denies all of this because it has been twisted and distorted by the interference of daevic forces of greed and a lust for power and control.

From the foregoing depiction we can clearly see how, as seen from the standard Western perspective, the system of Zarathustra could be seen as the structural equivalent of what is called in the West a "left-hand path system." It was Zarathustra himself who rebelled against the prevailing norms of his society, creating "new gods" — abstract philosophical constructs — and overthrowing the old gods. He created a system of revaluating of all values under the guidance of his *good mind*, conscience and rational thought. In the process of doing this he taught that each individual was a unique spiritual creation (*fravashi*), which was spiritually immortal from the beginning and which was destined for immortality in the flesh, but that in order to gain this Final Body the individual would have to undergo a process of self-development defined by the struggle of the Truth versus the Lie. The technology used to effect this struggle is the Magian art: magic and/or the living of an enlightened and ethical life. In the end, as in the beginning, the individual will return to its immortal and perfected form.

VI. The First True Religion

What is a *Religion*?

Many never give any serious thought to what we mean by the word "religion." It may shock some to hear that humankind did not always have religions *per se*. That is to say a spiritual message independent of specific cultural contexts. The spiritual life of the ancients was bound up in an organically whole construct called *culture*. When referencing ancient times we can speak of a "Roman religion," or a "Japanese religion," by which we mean the spiritual or mythological features of that cultural group. In the past what we identify today as "religious elements" were really parts of a larger picture which included language, arts/crafts, technologies, myth, politics, economics, military tactics, and marriage customs. When a person said: "I am a Greek," he meant that he spoke Greek as did his father before him, he worshiped Greek gods and goddesses, he lived in a Greek manner and was thoroughly part of a holistic construct we can call *Greek culture*. No one really challenged this universal model of human spiritual organization— not until Zarathustra.

Before Zarathustra religion was not so much a matter of choice. Now for the modern Westerner it is clear that religion is very much a matter of individual choice. In a world where people are choosing every sort of identity for themselves the reality of this world of choice is abundantly demonstrated. For this freedom we have the insight of Zarathustra to thank. But as with many sorts of freedom, with it comes responsibility. If we are free to choose, we are also free to choose badly. To understand our responsibilities as free individuals to choose our religion we should study the history of this choice.

Zarathustra's Insight

Zarathustra acted in part as a protest against the excesses and deficiencies of his own culture, but this was secondary to the more important matter of his *insight* (Av. *daena*) which indicated that the true and only God was the principle of focused intelligence, or pure Wisdom, and that all other gods and goddesses such as were worthy of worship were in fact also abstract constructs or prototypes of certain ideas secondary to this single great prototype of intelligence.

Zarathustra identified the deity with the compound name Ahura Mazda. This is a profound formula. The first word is usually translated as "lord." It is a word that is cognate to Germanic *ansuz*, "sovereign ancestral god." It is the word that becomes *áss* is Old Norse. In Sanskrit it is *asura*. The Indians tended to demonize the *asuras*, just as the Iranians did the *daevas*. In any event, the word means something like a governor, or holder or wielder of some authority or power, i.e. a lord. The second part of the formula is *mazda*, which means wisdom or consciousness— the power of the mind to create and be active. The word *ahura* is masculine and the word *mazda* is feminine. This phrase, Ahura Mazda, is not to be understood as two distinct things, but one, with two intrinsic aspects. It might be best translated Lord-Wisdom. The relationship between the two terms is very similar to the relationship seen in Tantric ideology between Shiva and Shakti. There *shiva* means "lord" and *shakti* means "power." It is said Shakti is the *Power* and Shiva is the Power-*Holder*. The ramifications of all of this explain why the Zarathustran deity is beyond designation as to gender, it is a combination of the masculine and feminine. In the dyad Ahura-Mazda is beyond duality. (As a curious side-note to religious history of the 20th century, the school known as "Wicca" could be said to have its deepest root in this theology.) It is the root also of tantrism and of Chinese taoism.

The essence of Zarathustra's insight was this: that the only true and real god is pure and focused *consciousness*, that all of the gods and goddesses of his people are but emanations of this god and that all of them can be conceived of, and understood as, abstract *principles* of mentality. When other thinking men were exposed to this set of ideas they were instantly transformed. They did not necessarily understand everything that Zarathustra understood, but they became somewhat better.

Once this initial insight was absorbed, Zarathustra saw that the world was infected by a terrible disease called the Lie. Every person is at all times confronted with a choice: between the Truth (*Asha*) and the Lie (*Druj*). The truth is that man is good, strong and immortal, the lie is that man is stupid, weak and mortal. The good is that which supports and affirms the Truth, evil is that which supports and affirms the Lie. The choice of understanding the Truth is possible for all humans of all races and nationalities. Thus the first trans-national, or inter-tribal, religion was established. **The insight of Zarathustra created the possibility of a worldwide religion based on the sovereign choice of the individual.**

At the present moment in history, if one were to investigate the religion known as Zoroastrianism, one would quickly find that, as a general rule, it does not accept converts to the faith. One must be born into the religion, much like orthodox Judaism which states that one's mother must be Jewish in order for one to be considered a Jew. So how and why did the Zoroastrian message go from being one of universal appeal to one belonging only to an ethnic group?

The answer to this question is really not all that complicated. In the beginning of the Zarathustrian mission the Prophet tried to convert any and all to his new religion based on the insight that there is only one God, that of focused consciousness and that this is the essence of Goodness, which created good things. This God and the good creations are opposed by Evil, which must be combated at every turn. Although Zarathustra gained his insight from within the pagan Aryan tradition of ancient Iran, a tradition very much akin that of Rig Vedic India, he broadcast his message to the world in general. Zarathustra, as we know, probably lived in the middle of the second millennium BCE, around 1700-1400 BCE in the eastern part of the Iranian cultural sphere. This we know from linguistic evidence based on the level of language used to compose the Gathas, hymns which Zarathustra himself composed and which reflect the language of this time period. Over time the religion spread out among many of the Iranian tribes, but because it was against the tenets of the religion to use force or coercion to convert individuals, the spread of this faith was uneven and partial wherever it existed. To convert to the Mazdan Way one had to embrace it consciously free from duress of any kind. But the main point here is that for the first time in history *individuals* could actually *chose* the religion to which they belonged. Before this, as we have seen, people belonged to the "religion" they were born into, married into, or into which they were adopted or made a blood-brother. In archaic times there was an identity between ethnic and spiritual traditions. There was Greek religion, Germanic religion, Japanese religion, etc. Zarathustra introduced the idea of individual conscious choice.

With the advent of the Persian Empire in the middle of the first millennium BCE, between 550 and 330 BCE, more of the world became exposed to the teachings of the Prophet. Archeological evidence indicates there were temples from China to the Caucuses. There is no indication of the restriction of Zoroastrianism to those born into the faith until well after the conquest of the Sasanian Empire by the Arabic Muslims between 633 and 651 CE. After that time it was forbidden to Zoroastrians to proselytize or convert others to their faith, because it was the ruthless mission of the Arabs to convert other peoples to Islam. It became a crime to convert to Zoroastrianism or to return to it after converting to Islam. Many in the remote areas of Iran remained loyal to the Truth. Clearly, however, these prohibition meant that Zoroastrianism could only be followed by those who were born into it. Today only about 150,000 Zoroastrians remain in Iran. As is well-known, around 950 CE a group of Zoroastrians migrated to the west coast of India. They entered into a Hindu world which itself had been under constant threat of Islamic invasion. The local Hindus could only peacefully accept the Zoroastrian presence if they kept to themselves as regards marriage and religion. Therefore, again, the formerly universal religion of Zoroastrianism was restricted by historical circumstances. It had to give up expansion and articulating its message to outsiders in a direct way.

These historical circumstances led to Zoroastrians adopting a policy of non-conversion of outsiders. This is generally the situation that prevails in the orthodox Zoroastrian faith today. Western Mazdans are not bothered by this situation. Zoroastrians have almost four thousand years of cultural development attached to their culture, practices and customs. For a European or American to "convert" to that religion would entail a complete re-inculturation of that individual— an impossible and undesirable event. Similarly and for similar reasons Orthodox Judaism does not accept converts. It is not only impossible, its partial success would only lead to disintegration and degradation within the orthodox cultures built over centuries of time.

The Mazdan Way is a religion based on the insight and theology of Zarathustra, but one which is suited to the culture and customs of the West. In a way, Western Mazdaism is akin to a return to the more basic and less refined early centuries of the development of the ideas of Zarathustra. We must find our own way to the Truth, with the aid of centuries of Zoroastrian tradition to help guide us, to be sure, but still discovering what it all means for us in our own authentic cultural experience. It is our position, and our faith, that this development will be greeted as a positive sign of the pre-dawn of universal renewal.

It is interesting to note that among the hundreds of traits, practices and teachings adopted by Islam from Mazdaism is the doctrine that conversion to Islam must come as a matter of conscience and not force. This doctrine is founded on the Qur'anic verse which reads: "If it had been thy Lord's will, they would have all believed, all who are on earth! Wilt thou then compel mankind, against their will to believe!" (Sura 10: 99). Of course the fundamental difference lies in the fact that Muslims do *not* follow this teaching in practice and do use coercive tactics, from the threat of death to the imposition of increased taxes (Ar. *jizyah*) on non-Muslims. Also, once one has chosen Islam it is forbidden to make another choice later. This sin of apostasy is often punished with death. Conversely, Zoroastrians really do practice the doctrine of non-coercion. The fact that coercion has worked so well historically is merely testimony to the power of Ahriman in the world today. The *daevas* work through ignorance, violence and greed to get their ways. In the defense of Islam it must be said that at least they give lip service to the Mazdan way of truth, whereas the medieval Christian church seems to have had no compunctions about using force as a first response to perceived religious opposition.

Three major religions which have a root in the teachings of Zarathustra and also have been successful in one way or another in converting whole peoples to their "religion." These are Buddhism, Christianity and Islam. It is likely that the very idea of converting foreign peoples to a new way of thinking regardless of their tribal traditions is a Zoroastrian idea. As such it is the world's first true religion seen as a cultural feature with some independence from the tribal cult. The idea behind it was the establishment of peace and prosperity and a reduction of violence.

The Persian Idea of Empire

The first true empire was that of the Persians shaped first in the mind of Cyrus the Great (died 4 December 530 BCE) and then enacted by him and his successors in the Achaemenid Empire (550 - 330 BCE). His model became the basis for all subsequent attempts to develop an empire: Alexander the Great, the Chinese Empire, the Roman Empire, Parthian Empire, the Sasanian Empire, the Holy Roman Empire, the British Empire, the Napoleonic Empire, etc. None of these succeeded as Cyrus had envisioned. To begin with, what is an emperor? Clearly the Persian word for this explains their vision: šahânšah— "king of kings." The Persian concept is one akin to a world-wide cultural garden. Each plant, as each nation, has its place in which to thrive in peace and plenty: the sun shines on all, the soil nourishes all. The gardener keeps the plants safe and well fed. Cyrus' vision was one in which the whole world would be managed by a great overarching governance, but each "kingdom," each nation, would be free to pursue its own culture as conscience dictates. The need for war would be eliminated because the emperor would ensure peace between the nations. His dream was to expand knowledge, minimize violence and maximize prosperity. He did this under the guidance of the principles of Zoroastrianism. Even the war-tactics of the Persians were formulated to minimize casualties for his men while making a quick end to the enemy. The use of archers and overwhelming force of numbers of men in the field are tactics that stem from a sense of mercy and kindness. Wars had to be pursued, but they did not have to be any more violent than necessary. He was often able to conquer whole nations (such as Babylon) through the use of psychological warfare with no violence at all. These peculiar Persian tactics would occasionally prove inferior to the bloodthirsty love of violence displayed by the Greeks. But as regards the concept of empire the key to the Persian idea, and idea usually ignored by all subsequent attempts to form empires, is that each nation must be allowed its own identity and perpetuation of its own culture— the ideal empire is a mosaic of individual nations, a kaleidoscope of lights working together and reaping the daily rewards of intelligence, tranquility and prosperity. One has only to look at the tiny "empire" of nations known as

Switzerland to see how well it can work. Four groups of people, each with their own culture and language, all living together in peace and prosperity: armed to the teeth to guard against any foreign aggression. If the vision of Cyrus sounds like something the United Nations dreamed up, it will come as no surprise that a copy of the famous Seal of Cyrus, said to be a statement of universal human rights, is displayed in the United Nations headquarters in New York. Again we see here a good idea run into the ground by *daevic* forces of greed, power and control. Inevitably we will move toward a global government, but will we follow the vision of Cyrus and be like the Swiss, or the vision of Hitler and be like the Nazis? One allows for and encourages cultural diversity, the other is the domination of all others by one. The good choice is clear, but who has the strength to make it happen?

From the inception of the religion of Zarathustra, the faith known as Mazda-yasna, "wisdom-worship," the effort was made to expand its field of operation. Zarathustra and the priests he initiated into his system, men who constituted the original Mazmaga ("Great Fellowship") and who were charged with the responsibility of memorizing the sacred works and passing them on to the next generation all sought to enlighten as many people as possible, regardless of their ethnic origin. Due to the unwavering principles of the faith, however, they could not use tactics of fear or coercion in the process. The fundamental belief was that Ahura Mazda was the one and only true god, defined as pure consciousness or wisdom, and that all people who sought wisdom, and thereby thought good thoughts, spoke good words, and did good acts under the guidance of wisdom were in fact Mazdans. The Great Fellowship taught people from many cultures, but the transmission of understanding was very often garbled with misunderstandings. The only pure way to receive the message in an unadulterated way was by absorbing it through the *manthras* of the Mazdan tradition. The religion, or insight (*daena*), spread from one Central Asian kingdom to the next and eventually was heard and accepted by the Persians and Medes in the westernmost part of the Iranian world. By the time of the Achaemenid Empire of Cyrus and his successors, the Mazda-yasna was well and long established. The Achaemenid Empire included some twenty-eight different countries, and it is known that there were Magian priests in all of them. This spread from Armenia to Egypt and Libya, from India to parts of China.

The whole Persian world was violently disrupted by the conquest by Alexander the Macedonian. Many priests were killed and books were destroyed. It was left to the Parthians, a people akin to the Scythians, to rebuild an Iranian empire. This they did by reinstituting and supporting the religion of Mazda-yasna. Only in so doing could they reassert their national character. This marked a new era of expansion for the religion, which was carried forth by the Sasanians, who succeeded the Parthians in 224 CE. It was during the Sasanian period that the religions took on aspects of an established *state religion*. This establishment solidified the institutions of the Mazda-yasna, but it also made it more identified with the Persian nation, which would prove somewhat counterproductive for future development.

In 633 the Arabs invaded and brought with them their newly invented religion of Islam. The Mazda-yasnians were persecuted and it soon became impossible to spread the religion. Zoroastrians were allowed to keep their faith, under duress, but they could not proselytize. So it increasingly became a frozen, ethnically bound religion. This situation was further exacerbated when a good number of them immigrated to India around 950 CE, where conditions of their reception and being tolerated by the Hindu majority was that they not try to convert Hindus to Zoroastrianism. So the ethnic restriction, already in place because of the Muslim oppressors in Iran was applied again as a condition of their peaceful habitation of land in India. These are the Parsees, and make up the majority of old-world eastern orthodox Zoroastrians of today. For the most part Zoroastrianism is a religion that does not accept converts. In the west there are certain groups and sects who thankfully do perform initiations. Chief among these is the Zarathustrian Assembly headquartered in southern California.

Other religions which spread out over many ethnic groups: Buddhism, Christianity and Islam all took fundamental precepts from the initial true religion of Zarathustra. All of these spread over vast regions and encompassed many ethnic groups. Buddhism spread slowly community by community with local monasteries as the vehicle for spreading the ideas. The Buddhist idea did not use coercion, and allowed for the continuation of native traditions in the various lands into which it spread. The original impetus for Buddhism may have been the teachings of Zarathustra on matters of silent meditation. Certainly the Zoroastrians reformed and expanded the Buddhistic method when the system arrived in Central Asia. This reform constituted what is called Mahayana Buddhism. This spread from the regions of the Parthian Empire in what is now Afghanistan to the Far East (China and Japan). Buddhism had been rejected in India, the land of its origin, as a backlash by Hindus due to the Buddhistic denial of the existence of the gods. Due to this rejection and exile, it had to make its way in foreign counties. It took Buddhism approximately eighteen centuries to spread from its point of origin to the borders of what became the ancient Buddhist world. Its separation from its homeland seems to have been the chief impetus and source of energy for its spread.

By contrast both Christianity and Islam spread through methods of deception, coercion (overt or covert) and violence. It took Christianity over a thousand years to spread in Europe. On the other hand Islam spread from its point of origin in Arabia westward to Morocco and Spain and eastward into the western parts of India in less than two hundred years. The Christians attempted to convert all of the inhabitants of the conquered lands and criminalized the continued practice of the old spiritual traditions, whereas the Muslims converted only a ruling elite and then allowed the effects of rulership (prestige, lower tax-rates, etc.) to take hold over time.

Because Zoroastrianism never completely lost its base in its land of origin, and because it can never use coercion to convert others, its spread was hampered. But those restrictions and historical conditions do not apply to the Occidental Temple of the Wise Lord. We are free to apply methods that will be effective, as long as they do not violate the non-coercion rule.

In general the Mazdan movement in the West represents a return of the Zarathustran message to its original spirit: it is well-defined, philosophically evolving, wide open to new horizons and accessible to *all* who choose to agree with its principles. We are once again entering into the old spirit of Zarathustra as an institution which seeks, and accepts into its fold, individuals who have understood the principles of the religion and who have accepted the major premises of the system, known as the Sixteen Guideposts. It is not necessary for members to give up their old religion or tribal allegiances. It is only necessary to accept the basic principles and to practice to the best of one's ability an increasing and ever-improving effort toward good thoughts, good words and good deeds. As the system increasingly proves itself to you and ever more fills your being with meaningfulness, you may find yourself becoming a complete devotee of the faith. This can not come with coercion or argumentation from others. It must come only though the application of knowledge to experience in the Mazdan context as understanding or insight (*daena*) grows. We hold that with insight comes transformation and with this transformation the need for rules, regulations and restrictions are radically diminished. The person will do the right thing in all matters because the individual *wants* to do it more than anything else. This is the truest meaning of religion, and the real meaning of the worlds *first* religion, that of the Mazda-yasna.

VII. The Nature and Problem of Evil

In our present modernistic day many people have become reluctant to identify something as being "evil." This reluctance has two roots: one lies in modernistic moral relativism the other in the Western confusion over what evil is and what its origins are. Moral relativism can be ascribed to spiritual cowardice. If one is reluctant to identify something as evil, then one is excused from opposing it. It has become the fashion to identify as pure evil things which are historical relics or things which pose no real and present threat, e.g. German Nazis or the Illuminati. At the same time real and present dangers are rationalized away. This allows those responsible for fighting evil to retreat and be inactive. Deeper than this, however, is the Western confusion about the nature of evil. Real evil such as ignorance, stupidity, violence, cruelty, sickness and poverty have been historically ignored or even institutionalized and promoted, while naturally good things such as intellectual curiosity, sexual enjoyment and techniques of transcendental consciousness have been vilified as the epitome of evil. The average Westerner, imbued with Judeo-Christian pseudo-morality, will naturally think of things such as "sex, drugs and rock-and-roll" when contemplating the meaning of "sin." This not only makes a person feel guilty for enjoying himself in life, which is a key component in tyrannical control, but it also allows the purveyors of the empire of ignorance, violence and poverty to impose themselves on the world.

Elsewhere we have discussed the Zurvanic idea that the evil god (Ahriman) was the co-equal twin brother of the good god, Ohrmazd. This is a myth that is easier to understand, but is not the myth of actual Zoroastrianism. There evil is seen as an inevitable and unavoidable, yet accidental, byproduct of existence. Just as shadow is a byproduct of light. produced by the presence of objects which block the light. Evil is likewise an inevitable byproduct of good, yet it is one that can be eliminated by the actions of Ahura Mazda's agents in the world: the *fravashis* of humanity.

The paradoxical nature of evil is discussed by Khojeste Mistree in his book *Zoroastrianism*:

> Evil in Zoroastrianism is not a reality in itself, but it is an existential paradox experienced by man, through the imbalance reflected in the physical world. It is only in the relative world that the states of excess and deficiency are observable and discernible, thereby giving an apparent existence to evil which does not and, in fact, cannot stem from any source.

> Evil only mirrors a denial of that which is existent and intrinsically good. Being parasitic, it does not and, in fact, cannot exist on its own. In other words, evil is ex nihilo, i.e. it arises from and out of no thing, and therefore it has no real existence. Nevertheless, it is observable as the denial of the mean which in turn results in imperfection within the relative world.
>
> (Mistree, p. 29)

This view of Evil as an absence of Good has a philosophical resonance, and was the explanation favored by the Greek philosopher, and crypto-Zoroastrian Plato, however, there is also something to be said for the idea that Evil has an existence and is an active force independent and contrary to the Good. The logic of this position stems from the fact that we can observe the presence of Evil in our world. Its presence cannot be easily denied. This is not only the evil that humans do when they make ignorant choices, but also the fact that unhealthy, degrading and ugly things exist in general. If Ahura Mazda has no part in this, which is the only possible conclusion we can reach if Ahura Mazda is all good and cannot create anything evil, and Evil exists, then someone or something else must have caused it. This other thing is the Lie (Druj) and its master, Angra Mainyu or Ahriman.

Relativists and others try to make the individual think that it is hard to identify what evil is. This is not all that hard. Evil is a deficiency of good, and an excess of any one thing to the detriment of other things. The Good is balance, the Good is many. Bad is imbalance and paucity. Most recognize evil when they see it, but may be too cowardly to allow themselves to be aware of it. This awareness leads to action and action leads to dangerous situations.

Most people can readily identify evil in contrast to good, if they allow themselves to do so. What is more difficult is to realize just how much each of us participate in this evil on a moment by moment basis in our thoughts, words and deeds. This often happens each moment of the days of our lives. All negative thoughts, words and deeds directed at ourselves or toward others are small victories for Ahriman.

I challenge the reader to set aside fifteen minutes, a half-hour and then an hour of the day simply to *observe* your thoughts, words and deeds and see how much of this is of a negative nature. Such experiments can open your eyes to the amount of work that needs to be done in order to reach an enlightened state. This exercise alone will not lead to the state of being as a *magavan*, but it is part of the process.

As the Good of Ahura Mazda and the *yazatas* is all really made up of abstract patterns, structures or constructs of benefit and balance, so too are the *daevas* of Ahriman made up of equally abstract patterns, structures and constructs which are detrimental and chaotic. Outsiders and non-initiates of the Good Religion may be tempted to think that the angels (*yazatas*) and demons (*daevas*) are thought to be little cherubs and hobgoblins flitting around us whispering in our ears and urging us to do good or bad deeds, speak good or bad words or to think good or bad thoughts. Such are the concepts of childish minds. Perhaps one must first think as a child before one can think as an adult, but the child's conceptualization is not the ultimate truth of the matter. In fact, *yazatas* and *daevas* are abstract constructs in nature (*getik*) flowing from the spiritual proto-type (*menog*) which are much like signals or frequencies and which tend to shape or deform our thoughts words and deeds according to the characteristic actions of these constructs. We interact with these patterns on a moment by moment basis in life, at each moment making a choice to think, verbalize or do things which will bring us as individuals and the world around us more understanding, power and prosperity, or more ignorance, weakness and poverty.

Evil is not a product of God, nor is it innate in Man, who is one of the seven great creations of Ahura Mazda. Evil attacks us all, God, Man and all the Good Creations from the outside, from outside our own natures. We inevitably live in a world in which good and evil are mixed. This attack on the Good Order (Asha) of the cosmos occurred before Man was created. The creation of humanity, by Ahura Mazda's combination of our bodies with the spark of the divine known as the *fravashi* and other divine gifts, is one of the chief acts of warfare by Ahura Mazda against the Druj.

As Evil does exist and is palpable in the world, it is only logical to conclude that the Creator is *temporarily* unable to defeat this Evil. If it were possible to do so, Ahura Mazda would have done it already. This task must be done, and it must be done by Ahura Mazda making use of his "secret weapon"— *humanity.*

What thinking Christian, Jew or Muslim has not contemplated his religion's theological insistence on God being three things: omnibenevolent, omniscient and omnipotent, i.e. all-good, all-seeing and all-powerful and been perplexed: How can God be all three of these and have evil exist in the world. Some have tortured their own minds and hearts into believing that there is no evil in the world, and that everything is just a matter of "perspective." Such is the spiritual refuge of a coward. Honest men who see evil know when they see it and know that it exists all around us and within our own hearts. Given that evil does exist, how can God allow it? If God is all good how did it come to be? Is it that he cannot see it? If he is all powerful why does he not destroy it? Logically, working though all of the permutations of these theological equations, the only reasonable conclusion is that God, the true and real God, i.e. the Wise Lord (= focused intelligence) is all-good (the essence of the deity), and all-seeing (as a product of absolute intelligence) but that Ahura Mazda is at present in a temporary state of relative inability to destroy the forces of evil. The answer of the

Abrahamic religions is blind and illogical. For the moment I will leave it to the reader to decide what the source of this blindness to reason is.

As to the characteristics of evil it can be said that it is a state of *imbalance*, a state in which there is too much or too little of something. The thing in question may be good and even necessary in proper balance, but a life-threatening evil in excess or deficiency. Take water for instance: It is necessary to all life, drought and thirst are well known deficiencies which have evil effects hostile to the good of life, but so too can an excess of water lead to death by drowning or "water toxicity."

In the our Germanic language the very word "evil" indicates *too much* of something. *The American Heritage Dictionary* provides the etymology of "evil" connecting it to the Proto-Germanic term **ubilaz*, "exceeding the proper limit." (p. 1547)

That these ideas do not have their roots in abstract philosophical speculation, but rather are refinements of deep Indo-European folk-wisdom is further shown in the German language, where we find the word *übel* for evil, clearly related to the word *über*, meaning "exceeding a limit," "over the line," etc. While there we also have two words for "bad" which refer to deficiency, *schlimm* and *schlecht*, related to the English words "slim" and "slight."

A general conceptual error is to see good and evil in terms of white and black. In fact both of these "colors" are extremes, either an excess or deficiency of either pigment or light. The good is truly symbolized as a kaleidoscope of colors and light forms, with each color or place on the electromagnetic spectrum having its specific use or utility. From a magical perspective, white reflects all and shields from all, black absorbs all and assimilates all. The symbolism of an even distribution of pure black and pure white is a powerful Mazdan statement. Zoroastrian priests in Iran can be seen in white and black vestments.

One of the most shocking theological realizations of modern Mazdan philosophy is that, applying the rules of logic to the relevant texts, the god of the Hebrews, named as the creator god in the biblical book of Genesis, must in fact be a *daevic* collective, and cannot be identical with, or even analogous to, Ahura Mazda, the Wise Lord. Among the many abstract constructs ascribed to evil are jealousy, anger, fear and vengeance. No one has to be reminded that these are traits of the entity known as Jehovah in the Old Testament. Ahura Mazda is logically, as the principle of pure consciousness and goodness, entirely free of such constructs. Once this is realized the behavior of "the god of the Old Testament" makes more sense as recorded in Jewish mythology. These realizations also make it all the more unlikely that the figure of Jesus could have considered himself the son of this particular "god." The Father to whom he prayed must have been far more akin to Ahura Mazda than to Jehovah. We say this because actions and words ascribed to him resonate far more with Ahura Mazda than with Jehovah.

The misplacement of evil in the West is a byproduct of the ambivalent nature of the conventional Abrahamic model of "God." This is coupled with a view of mankind that blames us for our condition, which is not all that encouraging in the effort to change things for the better in the world. By placing the blame for evil squarely on its true origin and seeing both God and Man as equal recipients of its deleterious effects we get a more realistic view of our task and our proper alliances. We need to be told and know the Truth before we can be expected to fight it effectively.

It is philosophically disturbing when we see people throwing around the term "evil" to characterize their opponents, or individuals or groups with which they disagree. This is a game usually reserved for the monotheistic followers of Jehovah or Allah, although many a so-called "pagan" often find it difficult to refrain from such thought patterns.

That which is evil is not impossible to identify: it is characterized by excess and/or deficiency and manifests the opposite of incontestably good things: e.g. wisdom, reason, strength, security, wealth and health. Anything which manifests the opposites of these and other purely good things, especially in an extreme way of denying vitality to them, or flooding them with contrary patterns or substances can logically be called *evil*. The ethical problem is that evil cannot be opposed by more evil, not in the reasonable expectation of solving the problem.

In order to aid in the solution Man needs three things: freedom, responsibility and education. The individual human being must be taught to be wise through a system of education in the ways of the Good. Individuals must make themselves secure and preserve their lives to carry on the struggle by being responsible for themselves and their fellow men. Additionally, individuals must be free to express their individuality and pursue their own destinies and natures as their *fravashis* dictate to them from within as they unfold or develop themselves. The forces of Angra Mainyu can be identified as those who try to thwart these processes, mainly by telling lies about them.

It is our task to identify evil in our own lives and in our own environments and take actions to stop it, speak words to counter it and think thoughts to deny its effects. The key to the process, and the hardest part of it, is the development of the skills necessary to identify and name it without falling victim within ourselves to the Lie.

VIII. Zarathustra and Islam

The casual unschooled observer may mistake certain aspects of Zoroastrianism for Islamic features. A modern American might even lump Zoroastrians together with Muslims. Nothing could be further from the truth. Zoroastrians were actually the first great historical *victims* of Arabo-Islamic aggression. Here we will analyze the links and distinctions between the *Beh Dēn*: "Good Religion" and Islam: "Submission."

Some people popularly say that Islam means "peace," or that Islam is a religion "of peace." But the word Islam really means simply "submission." The peace in question is that which comes with one's unquestioning submission to its absolute authority. As we learned in the historical introduction to this book non-Muslims were first conquered militarily and submitted or surrendered to the military leader of the Caliphate, who was also the religious leader. At first this was just the military conquest of the Zoroastrian Persians by the newly Muslim Arabs. The Arabs did not require conversion to Islam. In fact it was at first discouraged because their law allows for non-Muslims to be taxed at a higher rate. Therefore the more non-Muslims the Calif had in his realm, the greater his tax revenues. From the Zoroastrians the Muslims took a doctrine of non-coercion with regard to the acceptance of Islam, it was said, again borrowing a Mazdan idea, that the individual did not "convert" to Islam, but reverted to it, because it was the "natural" state of the relationship between Man and God. Nice doctrines, but not historically or practically supported, now or then.

It is widely believed or assumed that the Sasanian Empire of Iran was conquered by armies led by the Arab Umar between the years 633 and 651 and that thereafter Iran simply became a "Muslim" country. This is historically inaccurate, yet it has been made believable through a combination of Western myths and realities of history drawn from the Old Testament and the methods used to spread Christianity in northern Europe. The Old Testament tries to teach that the Hebrews took possession of the "Promised Land" by utterly annihilating the local population and replacing it with themselves. This is again historically inaccurate, but it was used, for example, as a myth for the manner in which Christianized Europeans spread across the North American continent. It is a historical fact that Christianity had spread in northern Europe in a draconian manner which involved military conquest and the subsequent and immediate imposition of Christianity on the *entire* population. The choice was simply given: *Convert to Christianity or die*. It was also part of the mythic culture of the northern Europeans that the population was automatically converted when the king of the territory converted. The religion of the king was automatically *de facto* that of the people, in theory at least. Of course, this also meant that if an individual did not comply with the royal conversion, he was not only guilty of heresy, but treason also! This background of understanding has naturally been projected onto the events surrounding the spread of Islam. This is the use of a misplaced myth.

When historical thinking breaks down, myth is allowed to hold sway. This is true on the collective as well as individual level. That myth should hold sway is not necessarily a bad thing. In fact it is the goal of Traditionalism and the natural spiritual state of affairs in traditional cultures as described, for example, by Mircea Eliade in his seminal *Myth of the Eternal Return or, Cosmos and History*. (1954) The overriding question is *who* determines the guiding myth and who gains by its hegemony. What the ancient Indo-Europeans theoretically had, and what they struggled to retain, was a myth which served the greatest good, which propelled the host culture to greatness and heroism, defended it against dissolution, and valued at the highest level the acquisition of wisdom and justice.

In the secular European Enlightenment the idea of a rationally based history as an objective record of the facts of human events emerged. This idea was promulgated as the ideal way to view the past. As it developed this proved to be a powerful tool in the hands of an educated elite. Armed with a factual, or more factual, view of the past, problems could be solved and avoided. The famous adage: "Those cannot remember the past are condemned to repeat it" (George Santayana, 1905) illustrates the spirit and utility of the Enlightenment view. This model, however, was historically precarious. Its full implementation necessitates the teaching of history to the entire population of a culture. This proved difficult, and in fact there is good evidence to show that the elite in the West, and especially in America, saw the implicit danger in arming the masses with this intellectual weapon. Generally quality educations are reserved for the elites in America, the masses are fed propaganda.

As myth is the more natural way for humans to think, it has proven rather easy to return the masses to a mythic level of thinking. But now instead of the venerable and ancient paradigms of Indo-European mythology being our guiding principles, the ruling forces of society, economic and political, have substituted an Ersatz mythology in which the gods have been replaced by film actors, pop stars and those who are "famous for being famous." While attention is diverted to these figures, the popularly despised politicians and CEOs use the new mythology, which successfully suppresses our true mythology, to empower and enrich themselves personally. Even most "educated" people today are much more likely to be able to give you the names of the Ninja Turtles than they are to be able to name four Italian Renaissance artists. This whole drift is, by the way, what makes the West so despicable to the remnants of the traditional world, some of which is found within Islam.

This digression on the nature of the question of myth and history will prove useful in our understanding of the way in which Islam conquered Iran and how Iran, in turn, reconquered both itself and and whole of Islam. After the military conquest of Iran the Muslims found it difficult to administer their newly won vast empire. Converted Persians had to be employed to run the apparatus of the state. Once these viziers were in place the re-Persianization of the country had begun. This was a pattern of historical behavior the Persians had mastered through the centuries.

The key cultural element in Islam is the Arabic language. The *Qur'an* is in Arabic only. Any translation is not really a *Qur'an*, it is only a "commentary." Muslims pray in Arabic only. All of this essentially indicates that becoming a Muslim means becoming "Arabicized" on some level. The Persian intelligentsia was always very facile with languages and dialects in the administration of their empire and the practice of their religion, e.g. Elamite, Aramaic, Greek, Avestan, Pahlavi and Parthian. The use of one more, Arabic, came as no great shock or imposition to them. Additionally, Arabic is closely related to its fellow Semitic language, Aramaic, which had been a long-time administrative language in the Persian Empire. These intellectuals mastered the language and even wrote the earliest Arabic grammars in order to learn and teach Arabic more perfectly. This was necessary because Persians soon began to compose new works in the Arabic language on a variety of topics, e.g. history, science, mathematics, astronomy. Works of Greek philosophy were also translated into Arabic at this time.

But when the Persians were first introduced to Islam after the conquest, they must have felt that it all seemed rather familiar. The reason for this is that Islam had actually originally been formulated by Muhammad under extensive Persian influence. An important book entitled *The Persian Presence in the Islamic World* details much of this. In fact it could be said that Islam was originally a reception of Iranian ideas and practices into Arabic language and culture. It is thought by some, for example, that the "man" or "angel" named Jibril (Gabriel) who taught Mohammad and commanded him "to recite" was actually a Magian priest.

The Persians had long been extremely influential in the part of the world that Muhammad came from. Arabians had made themselves very useful to the major empires of the age as masters of the breeding, training and management of camels. These animals were essential to trade all along the Silk Road, which stretched from China to the Mediterranean. The region of the Arabian Peninsula Muhammad called home, Mecca and Medina, were on the so-called Incense Route up from Yemen and the Horn of Africa. It was along this route that frankincense and myrrh entered the trade routes. All along the Silk Road Persians were the main economic force and were present in every station along the way. Muhammad would have been familiar with Judaism, Christianity and Zoroastrianism in addition to his own traditional Arabic polytheistic paganism.

The Mazdan Way and Islam

As we mentioned at the beginning of this essay, some outside observers might be tempted to confuse the Mazdan Way with Islam because of certain external appearances or regional symbols. This confusion would be a great error. As we have seen, Islam took many characteristics from the ancient Persian religion and culture, and in a way Islam seems to have been originally inspired by Persian ideas as they made a tremendous impact on Arabic culture throughout history. Additionally, the whole movement called Sufism owes most of its existence to Persian concepts and practices. In the beginning these influences were stronger, as time has gone on these characteristics became weaker. As it stands now Islam is highly restrictive, ideally bound by rules and regulations, generally anti-female and often beset by vague fears and anxieties. It was not always that way, at one time Islam was a bastion of intellectual freedom and innovative spirituality. Medieval Islam generally held the attitude that if a man met his religious obligations (mostly a matter of external behaviors) his mind was free to think as he would. This attitude changed over the years under the influence of Wahhabism (after 1700 CE) and other "fundamentalist" teachings, but in the glory days of Islam this was the prevailing attitude. For this reason Muslims were able to preserve and translate texts from Greek and Zoroastrian philosophy and make use of them in ways that only a small minority of Christians were able to do—until the Renaissance.

The original doctrines of Islam were already heavily influenced by Persian ideas. Historically this is explicable by the fact that Arabia, until the days of Muhammed, was a desolate crossroad along the Silk Road dominated by the Persians and Iranian interests from China to the Mediterranean. The region we now call Saudi Arabia, especially around Medina and Mecca where Islam has its origins, was a land so poor and devoid of value that the Romans neglected it and never tried to bring it into their empire. Writing was virtually unknown. The Muslims honor above all the idea of the *book*, yet the founder of the religion was illiterate. He recited the *Qur'an*, the very name of which means simply "recitation," to scribes, who were almost all foreigners, Christians and Persians.

Of course, as a religion, Islam was not alone in being shaped by Persian ideas: Judaism, Christianity, Buddhism and Taoism also received formational impulses from Iranian concepts. Because Persia was so rich in culture and deep in religious tradition and lore, and because the Arabs were so poor in all of these things, it was only natural for elements to flow from the area of high culture-density into the area of low culture-density. This was not just a matter of religious or ritual practice, but also of every aspect of culture, from architecture to music, to fashion, to state craft. Fundamental ideas that Islam probably took from Zoroastrianism include: belief in one supreme god, heaven and hell, angels and demons, end of the world, a final judgment, resurrection, five daily prayers, emphasis on helping the poor and rejection of the worship of idols. An essential concept of the Mazdan faith is that Ahura Mazda is the only true divinity and that the religion devoted to this deity is all of humanity's true religion. Islam took this idea and reiterated that Islam was the natural religion of man and that people "revert" to it, they do not "convert" to it. Also, a biographical fact concerning Mohammad reinforces the assumption that these ideas come directly from Zoroastrianism and not from Judaism is the personal association between him and a man known as Salman al-Farsee, "Solomon the Persian," who was originally named Dastur Dinyar. This man was so close to the prophet of Islam that he was considered part of the family of the prophet. The title "Dastur" may indicate that he was, in fact, a Zoroastrian priest. This close original relationship would also go far to explain why Islam was so open to further Persian cultural influences.

There are, however, also many points which set Islam at odds with the Good Religion. Unfortunately we do not have many texts by Zoroastrians explaining the differences because the writing of such texts would have just drawn the attention of Islamic authorities causing further persecution. Those texts which might have existed were probably among those which were destroyed. Islam uses Arabic which always points the convert to Arabic culture as being superior. Zoroastrianism uses Avestan which is a purely religious language and is no longer directly attached to any living culture. Avestan can therefore be a universal reference. Despite whatever philosophical stance the Muslims might take, the fact is that the religion spread by coercion, rendering it morally illegitimate. Islam saddles the individual with obligatory laws of behavior, Zoroastrianism teaches the good and leaves it up to the individual to follow his or her conscience to think, speak and do the good. We saw in the form of the Khorramis, followers of the "Joyous Religion," what post-Islamic Persians thought of Islam: that is was a sad and dour religion, full of deprivation and depression. They wanted to return to their ways of enjoying life. Muslims insist that Mohammad was the *last* prophet, Zoroastrians affirm that Zarathustra was the *first* prophet and that there will be a future *saoshyant* who will usher in the Making Wonderful.

Looking back on history it appears that Muhammad cleverly crafted an ideology and practice that was simple to learn (a few basic prayers in

Arabic), was an effective mode of unifying disparate people, motivating them toward conquest of their neighbors and profitably administering the conquered territories. The rewards of following the system were either an otherworldly paradise or one on this earth.

Despite whatever similarities might have evolved though history, the religions of Zarathustra and Muhammad are very different in spirit and essence.

In general the Occidental Temple of the Wise Lord is open to a cordial relationship with individuals of *all* other religions, regardless of what practitioners of that religion have done in the past. Humans make choices for good or evil every moment of every day, evil acts of the past can be put behind us, and it is individuals who make those choices and carry out those acts, not "groups" or "religions." Humans who think well, speak well and perform good acts are seen by us as Mazdans, regardless of what they call themselves. There is only one Ahura Mazda, a deity that all men and women of good conscience know in their hearts. Many call themselves Christians, Muslims, Jews, Buddhists, etc. — even atheists. It has always seemed irrational and stupid that people could say: well, this man is going to burn in hell forever because he didn't believe in Jesus, or this woman is damned forever because she didn't recite these words with enough conviction. Rather a rational God, which God must be, recognizes the Good in all who think it, speak it and do it. But our point of view is that the religion that understood this principle *first*, understands it *best*, and it is in the Mazdan Way that the individual will be most likely to find happiness devoid of delusion. In fact the Mazdan Way can perhaps even be a peacemaker between and among all of the religions that borrowed from it over the millennia. At least that is our hope.

IX. The Zarathustrian Nietzsche

Sils Maria [1881]*
*Hier saß ich wartend, wartend — doch auf Nichts,
Jenseits von Gut und Böse, bald des Lichts
Gnießend bald des Schattens, ganz nur Spiel,
Ganz See, ganz Mittag, ganz Zeit ohne Ziel,*

*Da, plötzlich, Freundin! wurde Eins zu Zwei —
— und Zarathustra ging an mir vorbei...*

The German philosopher Friedrich Wilhelm Nietzsche (1844-1900) is perhaps best known in pop-culture as the man who said "God is dead" and who coined the term "superman." He is much more than that, and in fact his ideas transformed the world in many ways and on a variety of levels. His most famous work was entitled *Also sprach Zarathustra* (Thus Spoke Zarathustra [1883]). This automatically peaks our interest and makes us wonder whether any Mazdan principles can be found in the works of this philosopher.

Some who have studied this question in the past have come to the conclusion that Nietzsche only used this persona to express his almost prophetic ideas in a rather ironic way. This interpretation is supported by Nietzsche's own writings, as we will shortly see. However, a deep-level understanding of both the ideas of Nietzsche and the Mazdan tenets reveal a somewhat different story. Beyond this also, certain facts pertaining to the development of Nietzsche's life indicate an intimate connection between the nineteenth century philosopher and the ancient Iranian prophet.

It is perhaps telling of a deeper, even esoteric, truth that Nietzsche himself said that his philosophical career was transformed when "Zarathustra passed him by" as expressed in the 1881 poem entitled "Sils Maria" quoted at the beginning of this essay.

Nietzsche tells us something of his attitude toward Zarathustra in his autobiographical work *Ecce Homo* [1888] in section three of the essay entitled "Why I am a Destiny." There he writes:

> I have not been asked, as I should have been asked, what the name Zarathustra means in my mouth, the mouth of the first immoralist: for what constitutes the tremendous historical uniqueness of that Persian is just the opposite of this. Zarathustra was the first to consider the

fight between good and evil the very wheel in the machinery of things: the transposition of morality into the metaphysical realm, as a force, cause, and end in itself, is *his* work. But this question itself is at the bottom of its own answer. Zarathustra created the most calamitous error, morality; consequently he must also be the first to recognize it. Not only has he more experience in this matter, for a longer time, than any other thinker—after all, the whole of history is the refutation by experiment of the principle of the so-called "moral world order"— what is more important is that Zarathustra is more truthful than any other thinker. His doctrine, and his alone, posits truthfulness as the highest virtue; this means the opposite of the cowardice of the "idealist" who flees from reality; Zarathustra has more intestinal fortitude than all other thinkers taken together. To speak the truth and shoot well with arrows, that is Persian virtue.— Am I understood?—The self-overcoming of morality, out of truthfulness; the self-overcoming of the moralist, into his opposite—into me—that is what the name Zarathustra means in my mouth.

Translation of Walter Kaufmann, pp. 327-328

Nietzsche's visionary period spanned from August of 1881, when he received the vision of the eternal return on a walk by the Lake Silvaplana near Sils Maria in Switzerland, to January of 1889 when he becomes either insane or divine in Turin, Italy. (After this time he referred to himself with a variety of "divine epithets" including Dionysius, "the Crucified" and Apollo.) Among his last works was *The Antichrist* [1888] which was a full-force frontal attack on Christianity. In an early section of that book, he writes:

What is good? Everything that heightens the
feeling of power in man, the will to power, power
itself.
What is bad? Everything that is born of weakness.
What is happiness? The feeling that power is
growing, that resistance is overcome.
Not contentedness but more power, not peace but
war, not virtue but fitness (Renaissance virtue, *virtù*,
virtue that is moraline-free).
The weak and the failures will perish: first
principle of *our* love of man. And they shall be
given every possible assistance.
What is more harmful than any vice? Active pity
for all the failures and all the weak: Christianity.

On the one hand his attack on conventional morality is clear, but on the other he does also clearly have an idea of the good as opposed to the bad. Nietzsche's robust attack on the weak, ineffective and powerless in life has clear echoes in the Mazdan sense of discipline as applied to the *magavans* and atharvans of the system. His attitude of being without compassion for the weak and poor is, of course, not supported by Mazdan philosophy. But even there the prophet of Sils Maria might defend himself by saying he lacks compassion out of a sense of kindness, for he says that this compassion or pity (German *Mitleid*) is akin to a deadly disease which kills both the object and subject of such emotion.

The comprehensive philosophy of Nietzsche is too complex to discuss extensively in this essay. Because of the visionary and poetic style in which he wrote, many different interpretations of his words are often possible. His cosmology appears to have been focused entirely within this world, on *Diesseitigkeit* ("this-sided-ness").

Perhaps most mysterious of Nietzsche's ideas is his doctrine of Eternal Recurrence-- *ewige Wiederkehr*. It was *this* idea which he himself thought was the *essence* of his teaching. Three ideas — the Will to Power, the Overman and Eternal Recurrence — are bound together in a triad: Recurrence is the law, Will is the method and the Overman the aim.

Nietzsche saw himself, and those who would *understand* him, as "Hyperboreans" — those of the ultimate north -- ones separated from the rest of humanity by their characters. They are to be *Übermenschen*, "over-men," those who have "overcome by going-under" (See *Thus Spoke Zarathustra* Prologue 1.) Nietzsche's philosophy is based on the force of the empowerment of the *individual* Will, or consciousness. It is a philosophy of *Diesseitigkeit*— "this-sided-ness." It is the individual, ego which is to empower its own will in order to become the *Übermensch*. This evolution into the Overman — this virtual "self-deification" — takes place under the direction of the Will. Essential to the *technique* of Nietzsche's active philosophy is the *Umwertung aller Werte*: "the Revaluation of all Values." This virtually defines a modern school of secular antinomianism instituted for the sake of the evolution of the Will into a unique and potent entity.

Jenseits von Gut und Böse

Most adolescent minds interpret this formula as indicating an amoral philosophy, one that denies the existence of the concepts "good" and "evil" so the individual is then free to make choices the only positive outcome of which will be greater empowerment, and the only negative consequences of which will be failure. There is already some nuances of mazdan thinking here. The individual human being is free to make choices, and each of these will have a consequence and is meaningful. A divine grace will not erase the effects of these choices. But when we reexamine these ideas we see that Nietzsche is not saying there is no good and bad, he is just denying that they are universal and conventional. That is they are not always the same for everyone at all times, and that they are not determined by an *authority* and applied to individuals as "laws." The authority in question may be a church, government or mob-mentality. It is the individual who is sovereign in these choices. These are profound considerations for the modern Mazdan thinker. The individual is sovereign and responsible for his or her choices, good is determined by effectiveness, and bad is characterized by ineffectiveness.

Wille zur Macht

The single lexical formula that expresses Nietzsche's philosophy above all others is *Will*. The English magician, Aleister Crowley, was no doubt influenced by this Nietzschean concept, and so much so that he made it the basis of his magical philosophy as well. The German philosopher was even more influential in the late nineteenth and early twentieth centuries than he is now. The formula "Will to Power" should be analyzed. The *power* is the effective ability to create, alter or destroy things, to have knowledge and feel pleasure. This is what the individual human consciousness desires and seeks and the key human faculty for the accomplishment of this end is the will or *consciousness*.

In many ways Nietzsche creates an extended commentary and analysis of the Avestan term *khratu*— "the unrivaled power of the mind to create, manifest, summon into being." This term is also defined as the "power of the spirit to triumph." It occurs twenty-two times in the texts of the Gathic poems composed by Zarathustra himself almost four millennia ago.

This will to power articulates and defines the individual being, the individual consciousness, which is another way of saying the individual *fravashi*. In Nietzsche's insightful psychology he recognizes that this will to power is the key to individual human happiness.

Ewige Wiederkehr

This concept, sometimes called *die ewige Wiederkehr*, sometimes *die ewige Wiederkunft* in German often also has appended to it the words *des Gleichen* so that the whole formula reads *die ewige Wiederkehr* or *Wiederkunft des Gleichen*, i.e. "the eternal return or recurrence of the same thing." From the moment it struck him in that fateful summer of 1881 forward it became the centerpiece of his thought. No one can contemplate it without thinking that it is fraught with mystical connotations. But Nietzsche saw it as a concrete reality. The formula recurs in his writings, but is perhaps nowhere better explained by Nietzsche himself than in a note on the topic published posthumously which reads in part:

> Whoever thou mayest be, beloved stranger, whom I meet here for the first time, avail thyself of this happy hour and of the stillness around us, and above us, and let me tell thee something of the thought which has suddenly risen before me like a star which would fain shed down its rays up thee and every one, as befits the nature of light. — Fellow man! Your whole life, like an hourglass, will always be reversed and will ever run out again, — a long minute of time will elapse until all those conditions out of which you were evolved return in the wheel of the cosmic process. And then you will find every pain and every pleasure, every friend and every enemy, every hope and every error, every blade of grass and every ray of sunshine once more, and the whole fabric of things which make up your life. This ring in which you are but a grain will glitter afresh forever, And in every one of these cycles of human life there will be one hour where, for the first time one man, and then many, and finally all will perceive the mighty thought of the eternal recurrence of all things [*ewige Wiederkunft aller Dinge*]:— and for mankind this is always the hour of noon.

No one can read this who is also familiar with Mazdan ideas and not be struck by the Zarathustran references: the happy hour, thoughts rising like stars, time stretched between two poles of limited and limitless qualities, the eventful moment of the noon-tide...

Nietzsche thought that the idea of the eternal recurrence could be proven scientifically, whereby all possibilities would recur as a matter of what we would call today the laws of probability, but he kept the whole concept in the realm of philosophy. All of this is clearly a reference to the Zarathustran idea of the final body, and *Frashokereti* ("making wonderful"). Here we have the most ruthless and austere philosopher of the nineteenth century coming to the same conclusion as the great Iranian prophet of almost four millennia earlier. Is this itself an example of the eternal recurrence?

Certain key principles of Nietzsche's philosophy clearly seem to resonate with the system of Zarathustra. These principles or traits are: a truthful rebellion against prevailing norms in society, culture and religion, emphasis on the individuality of the human being, action in *this* world as a key to happiness, and the idea that there will be, in the end, a *return* to the place where we started and that that place is a better place if we become conscious of the process.

Nietzsche's philosophy is not so much like that of Zarathustra's in details of substance or character as it is in its method. As he himself says, he feels that he is telling the *truth* of his age, the *truth* as he sees it in his vision, and as a truth teller he is most like the Prophet of old.

The last moments of Nietzsche's sanity are poignantly described by Paul Kriwaczek in his book *In Search of Zarathustra*:

On a damp and gloomy morning, the 3rd of January 1889, Nietzsche was walking near his lodgings in the Via Carlo Alberto in Turin, "opposite the mighty Palazzo Carignano, in which Vittorio Emanuele was born," when he turned into the grand Piazza Carlo Alberto, within distant sight of his beloved Alpine mountains, snow-covered at this time of year. On the other side of the square, in front of the imposing National Library, a carter was savagely beating his horse. The horse fell to its knees. The austere philosopher, who had uncompromisingly condemned pity as a debilitating weakness, sped across the road and flung his arms about the horse's neck— a gesture of sympathy and solidarity with another living being. It was his last sane and human act. He would never return to his senses again. He had finally passed beyond good and evil.

The spark for Nietzsche's grand vision began with a flash of insight rooted in the power of Zarathustra and it came to a close with an act of compassion toward an animal. These events frame the remanifestation of the spirit of Zarathustra in the philosopher of Sils Maria.

---

* Translation of the poem "Sils Maria"

> Here I sat waiting, waiting— for nothing really,
> Beyond good and evil, enjoying the light sometimes,
> And sometimes the shadow, everything just a game,
> Everything: lake, noontide, time without purpose,
>
> Then, suddenly, O woman friend! one became two —
> — and Zarathustra passed me by...

This is a fairly literal translation, but one that clearly shows that the "friend" is a woman, or seen as one (sometimes interpreted as Nietzsche's real-life lady-friend, Lou Solomé). The phrase "one became two" can be taken both as a romantic expression and an insight into the philosophy of Zarathustra.

X. The Purpose of Humanity
Your Mission—
Should You (Continue to) Choose to Accept It

Some of the great and eternal human questions are: What is my purpose, why am I here, what am I to do with my life? Most religions have some sort of answers to these questions. But they are in no way the same as one another. Are they all correct? This seems unlikely. Although they all may have a shred of truth, no thinking or right minded person would really wish to settle for anything less than the *best* truth in these regards. We will demonstrate how the Mazdan Way has the best answers to these and many other questions.

Most people reading this will have been brought up on a culture in which Christianity was, if not the established religion, an overriding cultural influence and determiner or religious "norms." It is therefore valuable to look critically at this established and conventional paradigm in order to go beyond it. Here we will be most interested in the various views of mankind. Once the patterns are clear and the truth can be grasped the right choice can be made.

As opposed to Zoroastrianism, which was conceived of and institutionalized by the Prophet around 3,700 years ago, Christianity went for several centuries without any fixed idea of what its basic teachings were. It lacked an established doctrine. It was the job of men called the Church Fathers to erect a doctrinal edifice. Chief among these men was the former Manichean, Augustine of Hippo (354-430). In the end he supported and created a system of dogmas which defined the Christian church. These teachings are:

1. The Trinity
2. Free Will (of God and Man)
3. Original Sin
4. Grace

The doctrine of the Trinity (that God is simultaneously one and three) was established by the Council of Nicea in 325, well before Augustine was born. Augustine accepted and embellished this illogical doctrine with three clever dogmas which put humanity in a no-win bind which necessitated, if one were to believe the dogmas, that man submit to the spiritual domination of the Church. The Church attempted to establish a monopoly on sacrality and salvation. But first it had to convince the people that they were worthless damnable sinners. This was done with the dogmas of Free Will, Original Sin and Grace. These work together as a package which says: Man's purpose in being created was to love and obey God, although this purpose is never made clear to Man. He is only commanded not to eat of two fruits in the Garden. Blind obedience is expected. Obedience is love. Man is endowed with free will. This was supposedly given to man so that God would know whether Man was truly being obedient or not. Other of God's creations lacking free will could merely be programmed to be obedient. But Man used free will to disobey God's obscure desires, this disobedience is Man's own fault and that *one* choice condemns *all* of Mankind to damnation as filthy sinners. There is only *one* way to be saved from this situation and that is by the Grace (free gift of God). According to orthodox Christian teachings promulgated by all Churches, when an individual turns to God it is not because there is some shred of goodness left in him — that was all lost with Original Sin — but rather it is because God has granted this faith to him by Grace. In short: Man is lost, it is his own fault, he is now devoid of goodness and the only way to be saved is through God's gift. This set of ideas was put together not to teach Man to discover the Truth, but rather to act as an apparatus for the organized Church to subjugate and coerce Man through fear, and often violence, to obey Church teachings— whatever they might be at the time. As we will see the Mazdan approach to these questions could not be more radically different.

These Augustinian dogmas are the backbone of the Christian church. Without them the church has no purpose or mission. *None* of the denominations of Christianity, neither Catholic nor Protestant, deviate from these Augustinian dogmas. Yet it must be concluded that these dogmas are in essence anti-human. The crux of them is that *humanity* (Adam and Eve) are to blame for the sorry state of the world. It is Man's fault and Man is in no way *needed* for the world to be made better. The supposed better world to come (the idea of which is a well-known import from Zoroastrianism) is in the Judeo-Christian system entirely the doing of God without the help of Man. In the Judeo-Christian mind to state that God needs Man to renovate the world implies that God is somehow not as *great* as he is supposed to be. To the Mazdan mind, however, Man is the logical partner of God. Man was created to act as the front-line warriors against the Lie. This is logical as only Man possesses the divine gift of focused self-awareness, intelligence and potential wisdom exemplified purely and absolutely in the form of Ahura Mazda. Man is not to blame for the bad state of affairs, only Ahriman and the *daevas* are originally at fault and both Man and God are their foes and victims. We do not only share a common spiritual spark with God, but also we are bound together in a struggle against a common enemy: the forces of ignorance, deception, weakness, poverty and sickness.

In this essay we will further explore the details of the divine purpose of humanity, its special mission in the cosmos, and the unique structure of the individual human being and its relationship to the divine world.

As anyone looks around the world today, or throughout history, we have to admit that evil is present everywhere. Forces of greed, poverty, violence, coercion, meanness, ignorance and stupidity reign in many corners and at the highest levels of secular power. This originated from somewhere. Did it come from God? Is it part of the true nature of Man? The Mazdan denies both of these possibilities. The worshipper of Jehovah affirms them. To the Mazdan none of the evil qualities come from the Wise Lord, whose nature precludes such a possibility. Man, as an incarnate physical being has voluntarily exposed himself to the constant barrage of attacks from the daevas on the cosmic battlefield. His weapon is choice, his mission is to win the battle by defeating the daevic forces with good thoughts, good words and good deeds. Evil does not come from Man, it comes from the environment of the mixed world of *getik* and the *choices* the individual makes in this world. The good news is that is our mission here: we need to be here and do this work in order to improve the world.

The essence of the individual human being is divine, defined by the *fravashi*. However, the person is most often ignorant of this reality. This ignorance breeds bad choices. By learning their true natures individuals can begin to make better choices and thus fight more effectively in the cause of the Wise Lord. By remembering who they truly are individuals begin to fulfill their missions.

The nature of the individual human being is to be free, conscious, mutable and destined for perfection and immortality. The individual is shaped and recreated on a moment by moment basis based on thoughts, words and deeds. A long succession of bad choices leads one in the direction of daevas, and the individual can end up being a "monster." His freedom was misspent. A life dedicated to good choices leads toward the realm of the *yazatas*, until individuals themselves enter the realm of those worthy of worship who are honored on the nineteenth day of the month— the *fravashis* of the holy ones.

This human destiny is assured because of the fact that the individual was originally created by Lord-Wisdom as a conscious and immortal being and that Lord-Wisdom will redeem all good creations by restoring them to their original state of being at the end as a logical and natural consequence of their origins. Because humans entered the fray on a voluntary basis, as an original virtuous choice, this destiny is assured.

A return to the myth of the Garden of Eden and the Mazdan myth of the origin of humanity tells a profound story. If we see humanity as the children of a divinity, we can contrast the way these children are treated and brought up by two different kinds of "gods." In the Book of

Genesis we read how Jehovah created humans out of clay and breathed life into them, then placed them in a garden where all was to be provided for them, without working or doing anything other than maintain their *obedience* to Jehovah. He commanded them not to eat the fruits of two trees, one provided knowledge of good and evil, the other gave immortality. With knowledge and immortality the subject of the process would become god-like. This Jehovah feared. So when Adam and Eve ate of one of the fruits they were condemned as sinners, punished with exile and the repercussions of "original sin"— they had to earn their living by "the sweat of their brow" (Genesis 3.19) and women would bring forth their children in suffering (Genesis 3.16) as existential punishments, for example. So now mankind must simply *wait* to be "saved" by divine grace. Jehovah did not *need* mankind, he only wanted them to love and praise him of their own free will. This was the reason he supposedly endowed them with free will in the first place.

On the other hand, Ahura Mazda is engaged in a cosmic struggle with the forces of evil — ignorance, stupidity, violence, cruelty, sickness and poverty — the battlefield has become a material universe, created by the Wise Lord to trap, confine and defeat the forces of Angra Mainyu. The Lord is all good and all-knowing, but is in need of a special weapon to defeat the Lie on the cosmic battlefield. This weapon is the incarnated *fravashis* from heaven, who became the men and women in the material world. Humans are the co-workers and comrades of God, needed to win the struggle against evil. The Wise Lord *wants* humanity to develop into knowing and immortal beings— this has been promised to humanity as a result of the voluntary act of incarnation.

In the first myth, man has no real purpose or meaning. In that of the Mazdans man is an essential necessity for the salvation of the world. If a parent makes vague rules and then punishes and disowns the child for his first infraction, and the parent never ceases calling the child an unnecessary complication, worthy of nothing, a damned sinner and a total idiot— what kind of person would you expect that child to grow up to be? We live in a world that is the result of the acceptance of this myth and image of mankind. The Mazdan myth stresses that humanity is the child, friend, colleague and comrade of its parent-being, a vital and necessary part of the strategy of the Truth to defeat the Lie. Man and the soul of Man (*fravashis*) are fully enfranchised into the pantheon of worthy beings in the universe. This parent has appreciation and respect for the child, calls it a pride and joy, instills in it ambition and a sense of purpose and meaningfulness. This child has made the great and noble choice of volunteering to fight for the Good. Now, we ask the question again— what kind of person would you expect that child to grow up to be? If you treat your students with disrespect and discouragement you get one result, if you treat them with respect and encouragement you get quite another.

Regardless of the ontological truth of the universe, when we look at these myths concerning the nature of humanity we see one that can only produce a bad result, and another that will produce the best possible outcome. The choice is ours. One dwells on original *sin*, the other on original *virtue*. Which of the two myths will produce the better world? Which of the two seems *right*?

Your purpose is to be a warrior for the good and right against the bad and unjust, that is the reason your soul volunteered to be here, even if your present form of consciousness has trouble remembering that. When confronted with this paradigm, you can again consciously decide to make the right choice and accept this mission and continually do so within the framework of the Mazdan Way. Once this reality is understood, the *best* choice becomes obvious.

XI. Z-Dog

> If those two dogs of mine, the shepherd's dog and the house dog, pass by the house of any of my faithful people, let them never be kept away from it.
> For no house could subsist on the earth made by Ahura, but for those two dogs of mine, the shepherd's dog and the house dog.
>
> *Vendîdâd* Fargard XIII: 9.

In the Mazdan religion the dog holds a special place of honor. There is no other creature in the universe like the dog. Other creatures may be more intelligent, stronger or more prolific, but none has the special relationship to mankind and hence to the Wise Lord than the dog. The dog is accorded special attention in the Avestan text of the *Vendîdâd* (Fargard XIII). The title of this book is spelled variously, and all are corruptions of the Avestan *Vî-daêvô-dâtem,* which literally means "contra-demonic law." This book is problematic for modern practitioners of the Mazdan Way for several reasons. It contains archaic and outdated attitudes toward the world and laws about things that are no longer a problem in the world. It is rather like trying to practice Judaism according to the book of Leviticus. This being said, it does also contain very valuable teachings on obscure aspects of the religion. As a field of study, the reading of the *Vendîdâd* comes very late in the training of a Mazdan practitioner.

In general the *Vendîdâd* divides creatures into good and evil and does all it can to protect and promote the interests of the good ones and all it can to destroy the evil ones. The only problem is that the evil ones are often misidentified. They are thought to be evil because of their aggressive natures or ugly appearances. As pastoral people the ancient Iranians had a special antipathy toward the wolf. The shepherd dog's special assignment was to protect the livestock from marauding wolves and from human thieves or rustlers.

As is well-known the Mazdan Way divides certain creatures into two classes: those created by Mazda and therefore good and beneficial in one or another capacity, and those created as a part of a counter-creation by Angra Mainyu which are characterized by their harmful effects on their environment. In ancient times orthodox Zoroastrianism ascribed far too many creatures to the evil class due to a lack of full scientific understanding of their function in the eco-system. It must, however, be remembered that the Zoroastrian religion, unlike most others, is open to scientific, rational discoveries and modifies its tenets accordingly. Upon one thing Mazdans both ancient and modern are in full agreement: the dog is the most noble of the animal creations. Of all of the Good Creations none is more beloved in the Mazdan tradition than the dog. Other creatures have a more powerful or archetypal role in the mythology, but none is so important to humanity and to the daily lives of humankind. The horse and cow are also of the highest order.

The official position of the Occidental Temple of the Wise Lord is that a creature is only deemed to be the spawn of Angra Mainyu if it has been scientifically proven to be of a negative effect on the environment and harmful to the lives and health of human beings, beneficial animals or beneficial plant life. Because the Mazdan Way is progressive, it is doctrinally open to evolution and change as rational knowledge develops. Our basic principles are those of the Sixteen Guideposts.

There are in fact many harmful and useless creatures in the world: fire ants, fleas, ticks, etc. Some of the things that harm us are so small we cannot see them, viruses and such. These serve only to harm people and animals. Their very existence is a proof of the presence of a "counter-creation" under the aegis of Angra Mainyu. It is a good deed to kill and cause the death of such vermin. There should be a scientific program to identify these pests and another program to eradicate them. But certainly all vermin which harm humans and dogs are hostile and in need of destruction.

The dog held many roles in the lives of the ancient Zoroastrians. They were important to the economic lives of the people in that they protected man's livestock and property, they were important in war as war-dogs, and in religion for their symbolic value and special relationship to humanity, but also in the funeral rites. The laws held out special provisions for dogs, and humans could be severely punished for causing harm to dogs. A folk-etymology for the Persian word for dog, *sag*, derives it from the phrase *seh-yek*, "one third," because the dog was considered to be one third human.

There were three categories of dogs: shepherd-dogs that patrolled and protected the land, house dogs that patrolled and protected the house, and the Vohunazga, who only lives to seek its own sustenance. This last type is a pet or companion dog and also the kind of dog that roams from house to house in the village. It is from this last group that dogs are selected to perform the *sagdîd* at funeral rites.

The ancient Iranians used dogs in their warfare and had what was called a *sag-e karzari*, "war dog." These would accompany men into battle. Presumably these were large mastiff-type dogs of the kind that can still be found in the mountainous regions of Iran. Their heads come up to chest level on a man.

In general the dog has special functions: it protects, warns, smites evil-doers, is loyal, dependent on man, and man can depend on his dog. Like man the dog is a cultural creature. It must be trained and enculturated to human society, in modern parlance, it must be "socialized." This aspect of the creature proves its high spiritual quality and kinship to man.

In Zoroastrian villages there are often neighborhood dogs who are fed and cared for by the community at large. Food is saved for them from the family meals and given to them as a sort of sacrifice. In the family it may be customary to save the last bite of food for the family dog.

The dog is an animal which obeys its master in a glad and joyous way. The dog actually derives pleasure from serving its master. No other animal is oriented this way. This behavioral pattern shows the way in which man should relate to Ahura Mazda. To follow the precepts of the religion should give us pleasure, not just from the rewards we receive for doing so, but for the pure activity in and of itself.

As we have seen, it was traditional in ancient times to think of the dog as part human. This belief may in fact stem from an archaic belief in reincarnation in which humans who had not lived proper lives would be reincarnated as dogs. It then becomes the community's task to treat them kindly, care for them, and train them well in order to prepare the souls for a new human incarnation. Their former bad behavior surely stemmed from unkind treatment from which they could not recover. Kind treatment by humans will help train the soul and they will return that kindness with loyalty and obedience.

In Zoroastrian funerary rites a dog, preferably a four-eyed one, i.e. one that has two dots over its eyes, is led before the corpse of the deceased three times as it lies awaiting its final disposition. The Zoroastrians believe that the dead corpse is subject to virulent attacks and possession by *daevic* forces. In order to preserve it from such attacks, the "gaze of the dog" (Pers. *sagdîd*) is used. The dog views the body and his eyes have the power to drive off any evil influence. The preferred type of dog for this service is a "four-eyed" Vohunazga dog, a companion or vagrant dog. A dog or dogs are also said to guard the Chinvat Bridge over which the soul of the dead cross in being judged.

The dog is important to the Mazdan Way both ancient and modern. Most of the dog's practical usefulness is a thing of the past, although there continue to be many heroic dogs serving mankind in various capacities, including the newer and even more profoundly Mazdan function of being "service dogs." But their spiritual role is undiminished.

Dog in Mithraism

The system of Mithraism, the fraternal organization active in the Roman Empire, indicates a special place for the dog as well. As our essay on Mithraism in this book indicates, there are no extensive written texts which reveal the lore and legends particular to this important and popular system, but the numerous art-works connected to Mithraism show the importance of the dog.

The most important icon of the Mithraic religion is the tauroctony—the image of Mithras sacrificing the bull. If the reader refers back to the depiction of this scene on p. 52 it will be noted that a dog can be seen licking at the blood being emitted from the killing wound inflicted on the bull by Mithras. Often a serpent is also licking at the blood, while a scorpion attacks the testicles of the bull. The blood of the bull is a fecundating, life-giving and creative substance. In some depictions ears of wheat can be seen growing from the wound's blood. The dog, with his master, is trying to harness this substance for the good, while the serpent tries to subvert it for evil. The scorpion is trying to attack the seed of the bull, which will be deposited in the Moon in order to give rise to further beneficial animals and plants.

In this image as elsewhere the dog is shown to be a help-mate of man. The dog helps man in work, is a fierce hunter and fighter and is a companion of steadfast loyalty. In the Mithraic image the dog represents all the good creatures who take their rightful share of the divine energy provided by the essence of the cosmic bull.

The Dog and Islam in Iran

It is well-known that Muslims are supposed to have a negative attitude toward dogs. There is actually no Qur'anic basis for this attitude, it developed for cultural reasons and with a special relation to Zoroastrian beliefs. These beliefs had to be countered by Islamic coercive practices which developed in spite of the Islamic tenet, borrowed from the Mazdans, that religion must be a matter of conscience, not coercion. Because the dog was holy to the Zoroastrian, and because Islam had to subvert and absorb Persian culture in order to become more than a marauding band of plunderers, Islam developed an antipathy toward the Persian love of dogs. To prove their love for the new "faith" of Islam Muslim converts had to show their hatred for the symbol of the love for his old faith, their loyal dogs.

When discussing the process of conversion to Islam by the Iranian Zoroastrians, Mary Boyce comments:

> Another means of distressing Zoroastrians was to torment dogs. Primitive Islam knew nothing of the now pervasive Muslim hostility to the dog as an unclean animal, and this, it seems, was deliberately fostered in Iran because of the remarkable Zoroastrian respect for dogs. Probably maltreating a dog (like discarding the kusti, or spitting in a fire) was a distinctive outward sign of true conversion; and the amount of suffering since inflicted on these animals by Muslims down the centuries is a sad instance of the cruelty that religious rivalry can bring about.
>
> (Boyce, 1979, p. 158)

Today in the Islamic Republic of Iran it is illegal to have a dog in your house. Iranians, aware of the traditions surrounding the dog have taken to keeping dogs and walking them in public as a sign of civil disobedience. Anti-canine Islamic attitudes really had nothing particularly to do with original Islam or its tenets. This attitude was a later development, probably, as Boyce notes, as a direct action against the Iranian love of the dog. It was imperative for the long-term success of Islam that it absorb the Persian culture and take advantage of its sophistication, learning and ability to govern far-flung empires. The Iranians had to be converted, and the mistreating of dogs was a litmus test of their true Muslim convictions, for no true Aryan would do such heinous acts.

This example of cultural practices which, although they originally had nothing to do with Islam, nevertheless become part of the essence of Muslim practice in certain regions is akin to Muslim "female circumcision." This practice is really a form of genital mutilation in which the clitoris is actually removed, and in extreme cases the vulva is sewn shut. This appears to have originally been an Afro-Egyptian practice which spread into Islam in a manner similar to the way in which the anti-dog bias did. Among the Aryans, only some Kurdish tribes practice this female genital mutilation. Although non-Qur'anic, such practices were adopted into the Muslim religion for the value they had in the exercise of power and control over people.

Good Actions

Earlier in this essay we discussed the fact that there are parasitic and harmful entities such as fleas, ticks, and heartworms. These were generated by the *daevas* to torment and harm Good Creatures. A call to Z-Action, to Mazdan Work would be the creation of local programs to provide topical parasite control for the dogs and cats of people who cannot afford to buy it commercially. Similar programs can exist to provide fire-ant treatment far and wide in the fight to eradicate this pest. These things are good and ethical actions in the Mazdan spirit. Additionally, support of local animal shelters is categorically a good action.

Perhaps someday the dog will again have his day in Eranshahr. The operation called *kên-e sagân*, "revenge of the dogs," is helped along with any support given to organizations seeking to return Iran to cultural norms as determined by Iranians themselves.

XII. The Mazdan Way: *Humata-Huxta-Hwaršta*

Here we will depart from the historical, mythical and philosophical tenor of the other essays in this book and delve into the practical applications of Mazdan principles. My other books on the subject, *The Good Religion* and *Original Magic* are heavily devoted to practical considerations. The essence of the practice of the Good Religion is said to be summed up in three Avestan words: *humata-huxta-hwaršta*— good thoughts, good words, good deeds. That is all well and good, but most people need more to go on than that to begin to practice this newest and oldest spiritual tradition in the world. Here, in as few words as possible, I wish to lay out the essence of what one needs to do.

It will be noted that there are twelve points to this curriculum, one for each of the normal letters of the Pahlavi alphabet, one each also for every word in the most basic *manthra* of the Good Religion, the *Ashem Vohu*.

Those of us who are actually working in the spiritual and ethical system of the Mazdan Way naturally struggle with what the three pillars of the formula Good Thoughts, Good Words, Good Deeds actually *mean* and *how* to practice the method. I hope this offering will be of some help.

Good Thoughts

Good thoughts are not merely thinking kind and positive thoughts about others or even one's self, although this is a part of it. More pointedly good thoughts are *effective, powerful* and *focused* thoughts. They are the blueprints for effective living. The thoughts are good because of their quality as well as their moral content.

To think well we must learn seven skills, or ways of thinking: meditation, concentration, visualization (imagining), memory, contemplation, logic and kindness. Each of these skills can be cultivated separately using various exercises, and they can be practiced at any time and anywhere the initiate desires. The goal is to learn to think this way all the time.

To learn many of these skills one can turn to the Internet and discover many sites that provide exercises in such things as meditation, concentration, visualization and memory.

1. Meditation: There are many kinds of meditation. But all are basically a form of an objectless stilling of the mind. You can learn to meditate in many ways and from many sources. It comes naturally to some. Others need to persevere. It is an essential practice of Buddhism, but was well-known to Zarathustra himself. The most basic form which should be mastered is the silent meditation without an object or specific

idea in mind. Simply sit in a comfortable way, observe your mind, and best of all gaze into a flame. Keep your mind free of specific thoughts, ideas, feelings or sensations. Your body and mind, or more accurately attendant *daevas*, will try to distract you and lead you astray. Simply and gently ignore them. Return your mind to its relaxed open state. Eventually you will arrive at a place of tranquility.

2. Concentration: unwavering, steady and one-pointed attention to a train of thought, object or sequence of actions. To concentrate is to enact one's will on a single direction. Your mind should be relaxed but focused on the object at hand to the exclusion of all other thoughts, feelings or sensations.

3. Visualization (Imagination): Like concentration, visualization is a skill to be learned. This skill involves being able to see in your mind's eye objects or sequences of events which you have created by an act of will. Some do this with their eyes open, some closed. This skill also encompasses the power of "positive thinking" — imagining what you desire and making it real in your mind (*menog*) before it is made manifest in "reality" (*getik*). These are the skills made popular in the video called *The Secret*. All great things must exist first in the mind, then in the world. It is the power of "inventive thought." Zarathustra was the first teacher of this kind of thinking.

4. Memory/Remembering: Memory is a complex faculty of the mind. On one level it is the ability to remember a grocery list, on another to memorize passages of text, *manthras*, etc., and on another it is the recollection of events of the past, both historical and in one's own life. Most importantly, however, it is the recollection of our lives in the higher, heavenly realm of *menog*. You should engage in exercises to strengthen the memory such as those found in books on the subject. Begin to memorize *manthras* for Mazdan ritual and keep doing this. Exercises to remember higher reality include the cultivation of attention to the **meaning** of the *manthras*. The ideas and practices of G. I. Gurdjieff are drawn from Central Asian models. Books such as *The Gurdjieff Work* and *The Master Game* are useful. This goes back to the craft or recollecting called *marethra* in Avestan.

5. Logic: Read a basic textbook on logic and logical thinking and argumentation. This is a weapon few have learned. Once you learn logic, you can argue better— not just more effectively but also better arrive at the truth of matters for yourself. You can make your points, articulate your thoughts, more perfectly. At the same time, and of just as great a value, you can recognize the illogic of the arguments of others and disarm them. Lies will not be very effective, crass advertising and political sloganeering will lose their effects. (This is why logic is not hammered home in public schools.) Ideally logic is the employment of the rational mind to arrive at true conclusions and the avoidance of illogic, which can be equated with *daevic* "thought." Now,

we recognize that *daevic* mental patterns are *extremely powerful*. This is because they prey on our weaknesses. The "cult of stupidity" is a real thing. Learn logic and use it and destroy the effects of this cult on your mind.

6. Contemplation: This is a complex process. It takes the five basic skills already discussed and brings them to bear with a definite purpose. When one contemplates something there is an object present. You contemplate a concept, a symbol, a myth, etc. You meditate *on* an object, you have a problem to solve, something to understand on a deeper level.

7. Kind Thoughts: By thinking kind and caring thoughts, and by thinking well of your fellow human beings and of the world as a whole you make yourself more effective and more likely to succeed in life. Make the world your friend and happiness will be closer at hand. One must also practice ethical thought. This is respectful of the existence of others. Ethical thought precedes ethical words and actions. Thought lays the groundwork for verbalization (and even verbal thought), and eventual actions. We must realize that whatever the *appearances* might be, all individual human beings are also animated by holy *fravashis*, even if they have forgotten it. Reminding them of this in *subtle* ways is always good.

Good Words

The average Joe might hear the phrase "good words" and think: "That must mean you don't say any bad words." Well, Joe is probably right to an extent. People who drop the F-bomb every third word are certainly not masters of *huxta*. But it's not because they are immoral, rather it is because they are ineffective or even counterproductive in their speech. To practice *huxta* one must speak well— effectively, ethically and be able to recite well the *manthras*.

Good Words involve recitation of the Avestan *manthras* necessary for ritual and religious work. The speaking of these formulas *out loud* is essential in this phase of practice. One must master ethical speech as well as beautiful speech: rhetorically and grammatically.

1. Manthra: Learn various *manthras* of the Mazdan Way by heart, the first ones to learned be are the Ashem Vohu and the Ahunvar, and then other manthras that are necessary for the performance of more elaborate rituals. The work of learning how to pronounce them, memorizing them, and finally reciting them regularly until they become second nature to you will be found to be worthwhile. When these are well performed you will actually be resonating with those who first sang these manthras thousands of years ago and thousands of miles away. You and they will become unified in a community of Truth and Order: *Asha*.

2. Rhetoric / Grammar: Pay attention to your grammar in the language in which you express your ideas. Learn techniques of organizing thoughts and words in ways that will be clear for explanations, persuasive for appeals, logical in the investigation of truth and engaging in entertainment. (If you didn't pay attention in Freshman English, it's time to revisit those lessons and learn them.)

3. Ethical Speech: Just as one practices ethical action, one should also practice ethical speech. This means speaking the truth, not tempting others to lie but discover the truth through honest inquiry.

As a note on the idea of *argumentation*: it is good to win an argument, to convince an intellectual opponent that you are right, but this skill should be used with discretion in religious matters. Do not try to convince a person of the truth of the Mazdan Way, present your ideas and let others cross the line toward you.

Good Action

The practice of *xwaršta* is synthetic, that is, it brings the other two pillars of practice into operation simultaneously. Good words and good thoughts are used as patterns of action and action is brought into physical manifestation.

We enact this pillar in two ways: in *yasna* (worship or ritual) and in mindful work and living in an everyday way. One is done in a controlled ceremonial and formal way, the other is done as we go about our daily business of living and interacting with the world and society around us.

1. Yasna (Worship): Various ritual practices are outlined in books such as *The Good Religion* or *Original Magic*. The practitioner should learn these rituals by heart and enact them frequently. The skills of concentration, visualization and memory are all brought to bear as the rituals are performed as works of art. They should be like flowing meditations of thought, word and action. Their symbolic and magical value are intrinsic and innate. The performance of ritual has become somewhat foreign to the modern mind, but there is something timeless and powerful about it that cannot be replaced with ethical thought and action alone. The word *yasna* means "worship," which literally means simply to give honor and positive attention to something.

2. Mindful Work / Living: The practice of remembering who we are and being awake, present and mindful in our everyday lives is another aspect of practicing good action: we are aware of and attentive to, our movements and posture, we are mindful of our environment and the living beings within it, we take care of ourselves and those around us in a hyper-aware state of consciousness.

Resources

Many resources appear on the Internet for the study of material of vital interest to students of Mazdan spiritual traditions. These range from orthodox Zoroastrianism to the languages and texts needed for the in-depth study and understanding of Mazdan religion and spirituality. This is only a partial list of such resources.

There are several resources on the Internet for orthodox eastern Zoroastrianism. These contain many insights and information which are of great use to followers of the Good Religion in the West.

For current activities and a running account of development, see the Facebook group page for "The Occidental Temple of the Wise Lord." and our official website:

www.otwiselord.com

General

A tremendous collection of resources including texts and linguistic information is to be found at:

www.avesta.org

A comprehensive presentation of Zoroastrian heritage, which includes history, religion, rituals, calendar, and so on, is presented by author K. E. Eduljee at:

www.heritageinstitute/zoroastrianism

The Circle of Ancient Iranian Studies has a website dedicated to the "understanding and appreciation of pre-Islamic Iranian heritage."

www.cais-soas.com

Translations of Sacred Texts

Older translations of the most important Zoroastrian texts are available online at:

www.sacred-texts.com/zor/index.htm

These are the three volumes of the Avesta and five volumes of Pahlavi texts published in the Sacred Books of the East series.

Languages

For those interested in the original languages used in Zoroastrian texts, Avestan and Pahlavi, there are excellent, often downloadable, online lessons and grammars of these languages.

For the study of Pahlavi as a *living* language:
www.parsig.org

    The Agha Khan Professor of Iranian, Oktar Prods Skjærvø, at Harvard University has produced a series of textbooks for the study of Old Iranian languages:

Old Persian:
www.fas.harvard.edu/~iranian/Old Persian

Avestan:
www.fas.harvard.edu/~iranian/Avesta/avestancomplete.pdf

Old Avestan or Gathic
www.fas.harvard.edu/~iranian/Oldvestan/index.html

Glossary

afrinagan: (1) a multi-part ceremony of blessing, (2) the prayers recited during that ceremony, and (3) the vessel in which the sacred fire is tended.

Ahunvar: Name of the holiest prayer or *mathra* of the Mazdan faith, it begins with the phrase "*yatha ahu vairyo...*"

Asha: A basic concept of the Good Religion. There is no adequate English translation. It connotes a synthesis of world-order, truth, right, righteousness and holiness. Compare to Sanskrit *rita*.

Ashem Vohu: One of the most sacred mathras which praises Asha, and begins, "*ashem vohu...*"

Wise Lord: See Ahura Mazda.

Ahura Mazda: Literally "lord-wisdom," more conventionally "the Wise Lord," and philosophically the principle of focused consciousness or *wisdom*. This is the one and true godhead of all humanity, first recognized as the universal divinity by Zarathustra though his insight (*daena*).

Amesha Spentas: Avestan for "Immortal Bounteous Ones" and is the title of the six archangelic beings created by Ahura Mazda (see Yasna 47.1) to effect creation.

Aryan: A term for Indo-Europeans, especially in the eastern realms. The prefix Ar- is reflected in Persian Er- or Ir-, as in Ir-an. It is not a racial, but a religious term denoting those who worship the Aryan (Indo-European) gods and goddesses forming a community of conscience. Zoroastrians also attached themselves to the term.

Atar (Av.), (Phl.) Adar: (1) The consecrated fire. (2) The *yazata* of Fire.

Avesta: Holy scripture of the Mazdan religion.

Avestan: The archaic Indo-European language in which the earliest scripture is recorded. It is similar in structure to Rig Vedic Sanskrit.

daena: (1) Religion, (2) conscience, insight, inner consciousness of self, (3) a part of the soul which stores the faculty of insight or self-awareness.

daeva: A demon, or pattern of destructive or ignorant thought or action, in the inner or outer worlds.

Fravashi: Often referred to as a "guardian angel," the *fravashi* is the heavenly archetype of the individual soul. It is that part of humanity that actually chose to take up the struggle of the Wise Lord against the forces of destruction.

Gathas: The 17 hymns composed by Zarathustra himself which are contained in the *Avesta*. They are in the most archaic dialect of Avestan, and date from around 1700 BCE.

getig: The world, material existence.

haoma: Ritual consecrated drink consumed in rites of the Good

Religion. Compare to Sanskrit *soma*.

Indo-European: Academic term for the common ancestral culture and language which is the point of origin for most of the European cultures as well as those of the Iranian peoples and those of northern India. The more Romantic and perhaps antiquated term "Aryan" can be considered an equivalent.

Iranian: Tehnically an ajective refering to elements within Eranshahr, language cultures, etc. Can be used synonomously with "Persian."

khwarr: Avestan *khvarenah*, Pahlavi *khwarrah*, this word denotes the "glory" of an individual. It is the divine empowerment and/or luck attached to an individual. It is increased by ethical and heroic action. This is depicted in Iranian art as a nimbus, and is the origin of the "halo" in Western depictions of religious figures.

magavan: Iranian term for a priest ("man of power") from which the term "magician" was developed.

magic: The art and science of the *magavans*. A system whereby individuals can effectively communicate their wills in the universe in order to modify or qualify events or states of mind and consciousness.

Magian: A popular term denoting priests and followers of the Zoroastrian religion especially in the western part of the Persian Empire.

manthra: Holy Word, many passages in the *Avesta* with specific spiritual qualities. These are verbal formulas which link the human and divine minds. Compare to Sanskrit *mantra*.

Mazdan: (1) Noun. A follower of the Good Religion in the new tradition of the Occidental Temple of the Wise Lord. (2) Adjective. Pertaining to the religion of the Wise Lord.

menog: The spiritual world and the prototype of the material world.

Persian: Adjective originally referring to a specific tribal region in south-western Iran from which the Achaemenid Empire emerged. Later used to designate the whole country of Iran. Can be used synonomously with "Iranian."

Saoshyant: A (World) Savior, one who has incarnated to bring and teach a new level of salvation to mankind. There are to be several of these throughout history, culminating in the final Saoshyant who will usher in the "Making Wonderful," or final Renovation.

Truth: See *Asha*.

Yashts: These are 21 hymns in Younger Avestan which praise and invoke specific divinities or concepts.

Yasnas: Avestan texts arranged in 72 chapters which are recited in the ritual of Zoroastrianism, also called a *yasna*, or "worship." The Gathas are embedded in the Yasna texts. Most of them are in the slightly older dialect of the Avestan language.

yazata (Av.): Literal meaning: "One worthy of worship," it is a technical term designating abstract principles and a variety of old Indo-European gods and goddesses who were incorporated into the pantheon of the Good Religion under Ahura Mazda. They are widely referred to as "angels" as they are transmitters of the will of the divine godhead. It is from this tradition that the doctrine of angels was developed in the Judaic, Christian and Muslim religions.

Zoroastrian: Noun or adjective. Based on the Greek version of the name of the Prophet Zarathushtra. Used to indicate the orthodox eastern form of the Good Religion. Sometimes used as a synonymn for Mazdan.

Bibliography

Axworthy, Michael. *Iran: Empire of the Mind*. London: Penguin, 2007.
Boyce, Mary. *Zoroastrians: Their Religious Beliefs and Practices*. London: Routledge & Kegan Paul, 1986.
——————. *Textual Sources for the Study of Zoroastrianism*. Chicago: University of Chicago Press, 1984.
Clark, Peter. *Zoroastrianism*. Eastbourne: Sussex Academic Press, 1998.
Clauss, Manfred. *The Roman Cult of Mithras: The God and His Mysteries*. Trans. R. Gordon. New York: Routledge, 2001.
Curtis, Vesta Sarkhosh. *Persian Myths*. Austin: University of Texas Press, 1993.
Eliade, Mircea. *The Myth of the Eternal Return or, Cosmos and History*. Trans. W. Trask. Princeton: Princeton University Press, 1954.
——————. *A History of Religious Ideas*. Chicago: University of Chicago Press, 1978-1985, 3 vols.
Ferdowsi. *The Epic of the Kings: Shāhnāma*. Trans. Reuben Levy. Chicago: University of Chicago Press, 1967.
Flowers, Stephen E. *The Magian Tarok: The Key Linking the Mithraic, Greek, Roman, Hebrew and Runic Traditions with that of the Tarot*. Bastrop: Lodestar, 2015 [orig. 2006].
Flowers, Stephen E. [Darban-i-Dên]. *The Good Religion*. Bastrop: Lodestar, 2014.
——————. *Original Magic*. Rochester: Inner Traditions, forthcoming.
Foltz, Richard C. *Spirituality in the Land of the Noble: How Iran Shaped the World's Religions*. Oxford: One World, 2004.
Frye, Richard N. *The Heritage of Persia*. New York: Mentor, 1966.
——————. *The Golden Age of Persia*. New York: Barnes and Noble, [1975].
Haug, Martin. *The Parsis: Essays on their Sacred Language, Writings and Religion*. New Delhi: Cosmo, [1978].
Hegel, Georg W. F. *The Philosophy of History*. J. Sibree trans. New York: Cosimo Classics, 2007 [1899].
Hinnels, John R. *Persian Mythology*. London: Hamlyn, 1973.
Hovannisian, Richard G. and George Sabagh, eds. *The Persian Presence in the Islamic Word*. Cambridge: Cambridge University Press, 1998.
Jensen, Hans. *Sign, Symbol, Script*. Trans. G, Unwin. New York: G. P. Putnam's Sons, 1969.
Jonas, Hans. *The Gnostic Religion*. Boston: Beacon, 1963, 2nd ed.
Kriwaczek, Paul. *In Search of Zarathustra*. New York: Knopf, 2003.
Malandra, William W., ed. tr. *An Introduction to Ancient Iranian Religion*. Minneapolis: University of Minnesota Press, 1983.

Matthee, Rudi. *The Pursuit of Pleasure: Drugs and Stimulants in Iranian History, 1500-1900.* Washington: Mage, 2005.
Mehta, K. P. *Our Heritage: Past and Present.* Bombay: P. N. Mehta Education Trust, [n.d.].
Merkelbach, Reinhold. *Mithras.* Maisenheim: Hain, 1984.
Mistree, Khojeste P. *Zoroastrianism: An Ethnic Perspective.* Bombay: Good Impressions, 1982.
Modi, J. J. *The Religious Ceremonies and Customs of the Parsees.* Bombay: J. B. Karani's Sons, 1937, 2nd ed.
Nabarz, Payam. *The Mysteries of Mithras: The Pagan Belief that Shaped the Christian World.* Rochester: Inner Traditions, 2005.
Preisendanz, Karl, ed. and trans. *Papyri Graecae Magicae.* Stuttgart: Teubner, 1973-1974, 2 vols.
Puhvel, Jaan. *Comparative Mythology.* Baltimore: Johns Hopkins University Press, 1987.
Rice, Tamara Talbot. *The Scythians.* London: Thames and Hudson, 1957.
Rudolph, Kurt. *Gnosis: The Nature and History of Gnosticism.* Trans. Wilson, Coxon, Kuhn. San Francisco: Harper and Row, 1987.
Shaki, Mansour. "The Cosmogonical and Cosmological Teachings of Mazdak." Papers in Honour of Professor Mary Boyce. *Acta Iranica* 25 (1985), pp. 227-243.
Ulansey, David. *The Origins of the Mithraic Mysteries.* New York: Oxford University Press, 1989.
Walker, Benjamin. *Gnosticism: Its History and Influence.* Wellingborough, UK: Aquarian, 1983.
Watkins, Calvert. "Indo-European and the Indo-Europeans." In: W. Morris, ed. *The American Heritage Dictionary of the English Language.* Boston: Houghton Mifflin, 1975, pp. 1496-1550.
Widengren, Geo. *Die Religionen Irans.* Stuttgart: Kohlhammer, 1965.
Zaehner, R. C. *The Dawn and Twilight of Zoroastrianism.* Phoenix Press: London, [1961].
―――――. *Teachings of the Magi.* Oxford: Oxford University Press, 1976.

The basic teachings of the Occidental Temple of the Wise Lord are outlined in the book entitled *The Good Religion*, available from www.seekthemystery.com.

www.ingramcontent.com/pod-product-compliance
Lightning Source LLC
Chambersburg PA
CBHW020205090426
42734CB00008B/946